AF480702

Cracked Lenses Breed Broken Dreams

Cracked Lenses Breed Broken Dreams
Rewrite Your Story. Reset Your Identity. Reclaim Your Future.

Nate Green

Published by Game Changer Publishing

Paperback ISBN: 979-8-90158-211-4
Hardcover ISBN: 979-8-90158-149-0
Digital ISBN: 979-8-90158-150-6

www.GameChangerPublishing.com

DEDICATION

To my children, Angel and Caleb, I love you both, and my life has so much more meaning because I have you both in it. The journey we have been through together has not been easy, but the hard times have provided many lessons. Thank you both for loving me and allowing me to grow as a father through the years. I know I have not been perfect, but I have done my best in every situation, circumstance, and stage of life to constantly improve who I am and even how I parent. I will be the first to admit that I have completely failed at times in how I handled situations. I have struggled with knowing the exact approach to navigate both of your spirited personalities. I have had to juggle circumstances outside of my control while doing my best to manage some of the crazy roads. I pray that you both know the heart I have for loving you and that I have always pushed to show up as the best version of myself.

Just like I encourage everyone reading this book, I would also like to encourage you both to always challenge everything you have learned from me and what has shaped your belief systems growing up. You are both built for amazing things, and the choice is yours to allow my shortcomings as a father to limit your potential, or you can break free and create your own story. I love being your father and guiding you, but know that I've had my own cracked lenses to confront, some early on and many over the years. This only naturally carries over to how I have parented, communicated, and guided over the years. Please know that I am excited for you both to spread your wings and take on your life journey to become the greatest versions of who you are built to be.

The story you write for your life is not about the life I have lived or the childhood you have had, but rather your ability to break free, challenge everything, and create the narrative for your life that will embrace the amazing person you are. The tough times you both have faced, the difficulties you have encountered, and even the unfair circumstances that have occurred are not what define you but rather only a part of the story that you both get to decide how it ends.

I love you both and am excited to be walking through this journey together. I am eternally grateful to God for giving me both of you. The love I have for you both is special, and each of you holds a special place in my heart.

With all the love a father could have for his children,
Your Dad

To Ashley, my wife and my love, you have been a light in the darkness, the hope in the rough times, and the heart when mine has been broken. I thank God that he brought you into my life, and I thank you for all your patience, love, and support. There is no one who could have been the blessing that you have been in my life. Thank you for all that you have done, not just for me, but also for Angel and Caleb. I know the journey has not come without the bumps, bruises, and even complete derailments, but you have been a cornerstone for me and have always pushed for love in our family.

This book has a special place in my heart, and as you know, I have had to work through a lot of trauma and past difficulties to be able to show up for you the way that I have needed to. I am praying that I will continue to work through all the cracked lenses that arise and continue to develop into a greater man, leader, and husband. Thank you for your patience with me and for the encouragement when I feel frustrated and burned out. There is no greater woman in this world for me, and you are the one that I know God has brought into my life for my healing, support, and to be able to experience true love. You are one of a kind, and our road ahead will continue to be filled with love, laughter, and incredible experiences.

As I know that we both have our own childhood difficulties we have come through, our relationship will be a testament to the fact that cracked lenses do not breed broken dreams when you have the dedication to confront them, reframe them, and seal up the cracks. The journey has not been easy, and I am sure there will be more roadblocks on our path, but I am committed to always driving toward you and willing to confront the cracks that form.

Thank you for being dedicated to our marriage, challenging me to think differently when I am stubborn, and pushing me to show up as who I am called to be.

I love you, Beautiful.
Nate

READ THIS FIRST

The dreams you once knew and the goals you've set for your life were never meant to be broken. But the way you chase your future must be met with a deeper awareness of the cracked lenses creating resistance along the way. These lenses quietly distort how you see yourself, your potential, and what you believe is even possible, often becoming the very thing that breeds the destruction of your dreams before they ever have a chance to live.

This is a seriousness we all must confront. You get one life, this life, and how you see it matters. Don't allow a distorted view of yourself, your future, or your worth to become the point of failure that defines your entire journey. You are not finished until the day you take your last breath. You still have the ability to rewrite your story. Stop chasing a life you were never meant to live, and start building the future you were created to take on.

As part of this book, I have included a Bonus Section at the end that provides access to the full video interviews on the resources page. This and other downloads will support you on your journey.

Scan the QR code here or go to www.CrackedLensesBook.com/Resources.

Cracked Lenses Breed Broken Dreams

Rewrite Your Story. Reset Your Identity. Reclaim Your Future.

Nate Green

FOREWORD

Leadership has a way of revealing what's underneath the surface.

When you carry responsibility for outcomes, people, culture, and vision, there's little room to hide. You quickly learn that discipline alone won't sustain you. Achievement doesn't guarantee fulfillment. And even meaningful success can't quiet the deeper questions that surface when life finally slows down.

This book was written for those moments.

Cracked Lenses Breed Broken Dreams is an invitation to pause, not to stop leading, but to lead with greater clarity. It's a guide for leaders and entrepreneurs who have done the work and carried the weight yet still sense there is more alignment, peace, and purpose available than what they're currently experiencing.

I first met Nate when he reached out to invite me to be interviewed for this book. What I expected to be a conversation quickly revealed itself to be something more. As I listened, I realized this wasn't just a book he was writing—it was a movement he was building. Getting to know Nate has been a genuine blessing. He leads with clarity, conviction, and heart, and he truly cares about people. In my years working with leaders and entrepreneurs, I can say without hesitation that he is one of the most grounded and intentional leaders I've met.

Leadership doesn't just require vision; it requires clear vision. We don't experience life, business, or relationships as they are. We experience them through the lenses we've developed over time. Those lenses are shaped by early expectations, past relationships, pressure to perform, taking on responsibility too young, success, failure, and faith experiences. When those lenses crack, even slightly, they don't stop us from moving forward—but they can quietly misdirect us. We work harder. We grow faster. We achieve more. Yet something still feels misaligned.

This book doesn't criticize that drive. It honors it.

Throughout these pages, you'll be invited to reflect on the expectations that shaped how you define "enough," the fuel driving your ambition, and whether your efforts are actually aligned with the lighthouse you're chasing. You'll be challenged to distinguish between motion and focused momentum, between performance and purpose, and between achievement and legacy.

What I appreciate most about this work is its heart. There is conviction here, paired with compassion. Challenge, paired with clarity. Structure, paired with humanity. Nate doesn't ask you to abandon responsibility—he helps you carry it with greater intention.

If you're a leader or entrepreneur who has achieved meaningful success but still feels restless…
who is driven but tired of chasing moving targets…
who wants to lead with strength *and* peace…

This book will feel like a conversation you didn't know you needed.

This book does not promise ease.
It promises clarity.

It does not remove hardship.
It gives hardship meaning.

And it does not tell you who you are.
It hands you the tools to become who you were built to be.

If you read this book slowly, honestly, and with courage, it will not simply inform you; it will confront you. And if you let it, it will help you rewrite the story you've been living under, reset the way you see yourself and your future, and reclaim the life that's been waiting on the other side of clarity.

When leaders learn to see clearly, they don't just rebuild their own dreams; they also create space for others to thrive.

Your influence matters.
Your clarity matters.
And the future you're building deserves both.

—Amberly Lago, *USA Today Top Influential Speaker, Best-Selling Author, Global Top 1% Podcast Host*

Table of Contents

Introduction

Anticipation flooded my every thought as I waited for the meeting that could decide my future. I had been notified that the chief of police had requested a meeting to discuss my medical situation and the future of my career as a cop. The seventy-two-hour advance notice of the meeting was rather traditional, but I would have rather had an abrupt, impromptu meeting, as the agony of the "what if" scenarios was eating at my core. The outcome of this meeting would define the next major steps in my life; this would be a moment of truth that I would never forget. The domino effect that could result might be good, good and bad, or just plain awful.

For the prior six months, I'd felt like a guinea pig within the medical community as the doctors had attempted to navigate my severe symptoms and determine the root cause and the probability of recovery. As a cop, you face many physical requirements in performing your duties, and one thing that cannot be allowed is a sudden onset of your heart stopping or resetting.

This meeting with the chief was to discuss the medical professionals' findings and their determination of my likelihood of ever returning to my duties as a law enforcement officer. The other part of this meeting was to determine the cause of these issues. If they were career- or work-related and I was deemed no longer able to serve as a police officer, I would receive a medical pension. The situation had gone beyond whether I could continue to chase my dreams. I was now engaged in a mental battle to stay centered as I figured out how to pay my bills in the coming months.

As I walked in to meet with the chief, the tension was so high that I still remember the somber look on his face. The chief was not the decision-maker in this situation but rather the messenger that the city had delegated to have the hard conversations. I could tell by the look in his eyes that my dreams were shattered and my life would never be the same.

He expressed his concern for my health and his appreciation for the time I had served under his leadership. Then he dropped what felt like two atomic bombs in my life: I would no longer be able to serve as a police officer, and the city doctors had determined that I didn't meet the requirements for a medical pension. To make matters worse, he said my employment would end that day, with no severance or any financial assistance from the city.

This was the worst-case scenario. There was no silver lining, no sunshine beaming through the clouds, only complete devastation. In this moment, I had no words, no emotions, not even a tear. All I felt was cold, hard, and empty, like I was frozen in time and waiting for my feelings to catch up.

This was the moment that obliterated many of my dreams and destroyed the hopes I had for achieving my goals. There is no way to fully explain what I experienced during this time of my life, and to this day, I struggle to work through the moments I had to walk through. That moment and the days that followed were riddled with hardships. Not only was I still working to get a true understanding of the major heart condition I was facing, but I was also now entering a financial crisis and dealing with broken dreams. As a twenty-three-year-old, I was dealing with what felt like a premature midlife crisis and having to work through more than what I had signed up for. The darkness of this time in my life required confronting the worst of thoughts and the hardest of realities.

Reflecting on those past moments helps me see how fragile our hopes and dreams can be. Circumstances beyond our control or prevention often intervene, shattering many dreams. This observation leads me to another perspective I want you to consider: how many attainable dreams become broken because of our lack of action, misconceptions, or failure to execute with proper awareness? To dig deeper, how many dreams do we fail to set or chase down because of the way we see our potential, our future, and even our skill sets and abilities?

I find it more devastating to have dreams that fall apart when I could have changed the outcome. As I have had dreams ripped out from under me, without any ability to change the outcome, I have become passionate about the need for myself and others to never let our dreams become broken. In your current moment, it is important to connect with the dreams that you have allowed to be broken and those that are still within reach, while being aware that, if you are not careful, they will shatter.

Each of us must recognize the three types of dreams that can be broken if we fail to focus our attention, build the right awareness, shape our perspective, and put the principles in place that support our development. The first type consists of current dreams: the goals, ambitions, future, and outcomes you are chasing in your life. These dreams are the ones you cannot allow to be broken. The second type includes dreams from your past, the ones that the younger version of you could connect to and may use for future goals. These dreams felt almost impossible then, but you were hopeful and, at times, maybe even confident you could achieve them. The third type are the dreams you never knew could be yours. These are the ones that haunt me personally and others with whom I've connected.

I am passionate about taking you through the process outlined in this book so that you can connect with them in your own life. What are the dreams from your past and the dreams you've had the ability to achieve, but because of situations, circumstances, limiting beliefs, and cracked lenses, you never realized they could come true for you?

This leaves you and me at a point where we have to face the harsh question: have we allowed ourselves to chase our greatest dreams, or have we only played it safe? Have we crippled ourselves and lost the ability to see the dreams we can reach?

The life in front of you will be shaped by the sum of your decisions. In the moments ahead, deep reflection and intentional awareness will be necessary. Right now, you're being called to confront the cracked lenses that, if left unchecked, can alter the trajectory of your life and limit your ability to reach your greatest potential.

I'm not coming to you as someone who has it all figured out or to judge you for having these distortions. I'm coming as someone who has wrestled with them, fought through them, and continues to rise above the limiting beliefs they create. It's taken years of facing hard truths and painful growth to uncover my real "holdbacks"—those limiting beliefs, resistances, fears, insecurities, and inaccurate self-perceptions—and to understand what it takes to keep developing into my fullest potential. Through every uphill battle and gut-wrenching struggle, I kept pushing, not just for my own growth, but because I knew the lessons I was learning weren't just for me. I had to be ready to lead others through their setbacks, struggles, and roadblocks.

I connect deeply with the following quote from Roy T. Bennett in his book, *The Light in the Heart*: *"The past is a place of reference, not a place of residence; the past is a place of learning, not a place of living."* Taking this one step further in my own life, I'm giving my past more purpose by leveraging it to impact lives and support others going through similar struggles.

I have arranged the pages of this book with a focus on helping you uncover or rekindle the dreams that your future could be filled with. It will help you connect with the dreams you are more than capable of achieving and give you hope to continue on your journey toward the future that lies ahead. The life you are hungry to chase after can be yours, and the reality you can find yourself in is far beyond what you can currently imagine.

I wrote this book to be a catalyst in your journey and to bring awareness and a new perspective to your life. I will be the first to admit that much of this book explores difficult topics and deep, thought-provoking concepts. All of this is included to guide you in the growth you need to gain the rewards that can only be found by fighting through the difficulties life brings. I have a passion to help you break free from the limiting beliefs, cracked lenses, and other setbacks that, if not recognized and corrected, will cause you future broken dreams. This book will connect you to principles that will help you reach new heights. It will also help you break free from where you are stuck and offer hope if you are burned out and exhausted.

As you sit in this moment, your moment, facing your own reality and mental setbacks, I encourage you to keep pushing no matter what. I am not talking about continuing to take the same actions you have been taking, but rather pushing yourself to keep growing and developing. Many people have given up hope on their journey and let their dreams become broken, but that cannot be the life you allow yourself to live. You cannot allow the regrets and failures that haunt your memories to plague your future.

You are built to take on great things. You are capable of so much, and you are only at the starting line, waiting for the "holdbacks" to be released so you can thrive in your race. These moments, even the darkest of them, are a part of your story, but do not let them define the ending of your story or the dreams that should be in front of you.

The most important step in this phase of your life is to become aware of those limiting beliefs that keep you from running full speed into the greatness that you can have. This all starts with how you see yourself and the potential you have deep inside. As Brian Tracy, known for his best-selling books and dynamic motivational speaking, passionately states, *"You begin to fly when you let go of self-limiting beliefs and allow your mind and aspirations to rise to greater heights."*

The journey is not easy; your future requires growth and dedication. The dreams for your future must be yours, developed out of hope and filled with clarity about who you are built to become. Your goals, ambitions, and aspirations should be free of the unhealthy limits that haunt your dreams. Your future self relies on you, in this moment, to dig in, push deep, and work to overcome the cracked lenses in your life so you are ready to not just face the life in front of you but to chase the greatest life that can be yours.

If you are in what feels like an impossible hardship or difficulty, it is important to remember that the circumstances you are in do not define you. How you handle yourself and what you choose to do in tough moments define you. Decide to chase after a greater future and then take consistent, daily steps toward the greatness you are capable of achieving.

I know that some of you might be thinking, *Nate, you just don't understand,* and others of you might be having racing thoughts filled with doubts and fears. To all of you, now is the time to take a step back and realize this is only the introduction of the book; you are not supposed to have it all figured out yet. There is a reason why this is called a "journey" and not a "destination." The process of becoming the greatest you are capable of will take your entire life. The most incredible journey that we will ever take is the life that we are living. Knowing that we have the ability to unlock growth, development, and a greater future for ourselves should inspire each one of us to lock in and dig deeper.

Through this book and the process I will walk you through, I want you to know that I understand this will not be easy, and the life you are living is probably filled with challenges and hardships. I also know that much of the reflection and work I will encourage you to do will bring its own level of difficulty, but you are not alone. There are others who have been through this or are struggling right now as well. You have to connect to the fact that you are stronger than you can imagine and are built to take on more than you might "feel" you can handle. This is why I take the time to open up and be honest about the hardships I have faced and why I strive to be vulnerable about the realities I have walked through.

As part of encouraging and supporting you on your journey, I took a step back and recognized that my story, my journey, and my hardships might not relate to each and every one of you. This book is not about me, but rather about you and how I can provide you with the most support and hope right now. I turned to my network of impact-focused people, who all have stories of overcoming adversity and hardships, and brought together an incredible opportunity for each of you to hear and connect to their stories. These incredible individuals provide stories of walking through the fire, facing their limiting beliefs, and overcoming their cracked lenses.

You will see a QR code below that provides access to all the interview recordings with these people. This is provided so that as you work through this book and face your own limiting beliefs, mental hardships, and major life challenges, you can gain inspiration from those who have gone before and pushed past their holdbacks to chase their dreams.

In some cases, the lives these people have lived have been marked by extreme adversity. Through their constant dedication to growth, development, and impact, these people have beaten the odds and accomplished great things while having a heart for others. This group has taken their time to dig deep into their past, discuss their hardships, and even explore the cracked lenses that have shown up throughout their lives.

This impact-focused project presents real-life situations for those who have been in dark places and have been able to battle forward despite the mental anguish they encountered. This group has come together to provide encouragement and support by sharing their real-life experiences, helping you connect and draw hope from them.

There are many names you will recognize and others with stories that deserve attention, as they are a light in the darkness. Some of the incredibly high-performing and highly motivated people who have taken the time to be part of this impact project include Amberly Lago, Ben Newman, Chris Welton, Drew Davis, Jaime Elizondo, Kristen Butler, Laura Casselman, Renee Marino, and Ted Rath.

In the last section of this book, the Bonus Content, you will find details about each person who has been a part of this project, an inspirational quote, an encouragement for your journey, and a challenge from every one of them. This is only the start, as the free resources that come with this book include the full podcast-style interview with each participant.

Scan the QR code below, and you will be able to access all the interviews:

Get Locked In

As you read this book, lock in and decide to break free from the limiting beliefs and excuses that have kept you anchored to your past and away from your greatest potential. The life that you are built to chase after and the achievements you are made to conquer are greater than you could ever have imagined.

Now, find hope in the fact that you are beginning this journey and moving to create change in your life. You are in control of the next steps in your life, and I am here as a guide to help you see the truth of who you are and cast a vision for your future. This is the moment you must decide to take control of the controllables in your life and push into taking action that will lead you to success.

The days and weeks ahead will connect you to the cracked lenses that have been derailing your outcomes and dismantling your dreams. The roadmap I have created for you will equip you to confront, reframe, and navigate these tough waters. For those who act, the principles in this book will be the catalyst for your journey and the gateway to an entirely new outlook on your dreams.

CHAPTER 1

Cracked Doesn't Mean Broken

The drill instructor was screaming in my face, telling me to give up, saying I didn't have what it took, and mocking every attribute that didn't meet perfection. This took me back to my childhood when my tormentor was ruthless and relentless. The drill instructors salted the wounds, knowing how difficult I was having with the intensive legal courses. This had given them even more ammunition to cut deep and the drive to inspire me to give up.

This strategy was put in place to "cut the fat" and get rid of recruits who weren't ready and those who would never make it on the streets. In those moments, all I could think was: *I can take anything for a season. There's no way I'm giving up today.* What they were inflicting would never break me; no suffering they could put me through would ever push me to a point where I would give up.

This pressure persisted day after day as I improved my performance both physically and academically. I have never been gifted when it comes to academic learning, as I struggle with what has now been identified as ADHD. Throughout my childhood, this surfaced in many ways, but luckily, I had a very patient, kind, and caring mother who provided me with a lot of additional support during my learning.

I faced major academic hurdles in the police academy that were used against me in the harassment of the drill instructors, as well as through the relentless pressure from the professors. There were expectations placed on me from the moment I walked in; I was the youngest to be allowed into that police academy to that date. They had made an exception for me because of my ability to communicate, convincing them that I would outwork everyone and give everything I had to ensure successful completion. This added tremendous weight to my shoulders while increasing the target on my back, as the leaders and other participants sought to prove the need for age requirements.

Every time those drill instructors would scream, put me down, focus on my inadequacies, and push harder into my weaknesses, I couldn't help but allow self-doubt to creep in. Was my older brother correct when he told me I would never succeed, always fail, and wouldn't amount to anything? There was an age difference of about five years between us, as well as a massive size difference and strength differential, which he reminded me of day after day.

I remember being pinned to the ground, taking knees to my side, and screaming for help, but the only one there to listen was my sister, who was even more afraid of my brother than I was. The relentless approach taken to break me and my spirit regularly might not have been successful, but the damage inflicted created a distorted view of who I was and what I was capable of achieving.

Those messages from my brother were drilled into me both mentally and physically, but the one thing they did was give me a massive drive to fight back. You can only imagine how much I was triggered and how badly I wanted to go after these drill instructors, but I knew the only way to prove them wrong was to become the best. The days that followed required me to lock in and to take extreme measures to buckle down on my learning and my physical conditioning. I would not allow them to dictate my future; I would not allow them to be right.

This participation in the police academy, during which I worked full-time, required me to have sleepless nights, dedicated learning sessions, and a relentless drive to better myself. This was the first time in my life that I had to tap into an entirely new level of grit and endurance. The biggest obstacle I had to overcome during this phase of my life was the mental barriers: the memories, the deep-rooted misconceptions I had allowed myself to believe, and the torment I had encountered in the earlier days of my life haunted me.

The hard reality of how discombobulated my thoughts, mindsets, and other ingrained aspects of how I viewed myself and what I was capable of facing came rushing in. This was the first time that they had become a major setback, a crippling power, or even fully known to me. I knew I had deep-rooted issues inside that I wrestled with, always feeling inadequate and extremely self-conscious. I just didn't realize the full impact of what had happened in my childhood until I focused on chasing my dreams.

I could either allow these false beliefs, which felt so real, to win or let the drive for a greater future take the lead. My life, just like so many of yours, suffered from the haunting effects of childhood, hardships, and other life experiences. These create what I call "cracked lenses," which affect how we see ourselves, our future, our abilities, and the opportunities we think we can pursue.

This season created a massive disruption in my mental life; I had to overcome hurdles and obstacles I didn't ever realize I would have to confront. At times, I felt as though I were damaged goods and wouldn't be able to achieve any type of success. The reality, though, was how much stronger, better, and more capable I was becoming because I didn't allow these things to break me.

I rose to the demand and became more relentless. I dug deep and found more resilience. I set my target not only on surviving and completing the police academy but also on becoming one of the squad leaders during my training. I did this to push myself beyond just the acceptable limits. To qualify as a squad leader, you had to rise to the top of the class when it came to academics. To be honest with you, I wanted to see the look on the others' faces when I got the promotion to the leadership role as their squad leader, the youngest ever to earn it.

During this period of my life, I had to set expectations for how I would show up and push myself to a higher standard because I knew I was capable of rising to a greater level if I locked in and pushed myself to extremes. The limitations set by others were not going to be my guiding light or the parameters for my success. I was now locked in on understanding the battles that I would face, but I knew I had to take ownership of every thought I had. The past and even the current situation I found myself in were not going to define who I was; rather, I had the ability to create and control the narrative by the way I showed up.

As I work to connect you to examples and situations I have dealt with in my life, I am focused on bridging the gap to the real-life situations you may have encountered or are currently encountering. I understand that your situation is not the same as mine, and I will never claim to fully understand what you are dealing with. The one thing I will emphasize is that you will face many difficult situations, challenges, and traumas caused by other people, but they cannot define your story; they are only a part of it. There are moments when you may have been, or will be, defeated, crushed, and even almost destroyed, but it is important to know that you are not broken.

Yes, the past you have had to live through, and even the moments you find yourself in now, feel relentless and interlaced with damaging side effects. This doesn't mean you have to let them define the rest of your life. I understand the mental battles, daily hardships, and haunting memories of past traumas, but they can never be the reason you settle in your life.

This is where awareness of what has happened, acceptance of what cannot be changed, and the decision to refuse it as the final defining factor create a true turning point in your life. You have to become aware of the cracks that have formed, can form, and will form because of the life situations and circumstances you have encountered. This takes you intentionally addressing them and focusing on how to move forward to become the greatest version of who you were made to be.

A Little Nerdy

As we walk this journey together, we will explore the mindsets, vantage points, and perspectives shaping how you see your life, your future, and yourself. These lenses influence every decision you make and every direction you take.

Before we go further, it's important to understand the concept of cracked lenses. Doing so will help you connect to how these can affect your life and even devastate your dreams if you do not properly acknowledge and take action to overcome them or seal them up. I feel it is important to first take you through a brief technical aspect so you understand that this isn't just something that I thought up or created.

When I discuss "cracked lenses," I am moving through the neuroscientific concepts that are known as "cognitive biases." There are many aspects to consider, including the types of cognitive biases that can have major effects on our lives and how we view ourselves, process information, and even take action. If you spend any time researching cognitive biases, you will find types such as confirmation bias, attentional bias, anchoring bias, optimism bias, the false consensus effect, and many more.

Researchers have extensively studied this list, along with related topics like automaticity and heuristics. I have devoted countless hours to studying these concepts and related studies, as I have found them of extreme importance in the journey toward success, achievement, and even personal satisfaction. These can all have a major impact on our perception of the things around us, including how we see ourselves, how we show up, and how we take action. These can have a major impact on how we see our potential and future and on how we react to every situation we encounter.

The cognitive biases and other related factors each of us faces can trigger automatic responses to situations, circumstances, experiences, words, sayings, environments, specific people, and much more. Even heuristics, which are mental shortcuts that can be conscious or unconscious, rely on prior programming and previous execution. These are even formed on the basis of inaccurate beliefs and ineffective action steps. The reason this is important is that these cognitive biases and heuristics are formed throughout our lives, many at a young age, and have a major impact on the decisions, feelings, and actions we take. These are shaped by the things we saw, heard, felt, and experienced throughout our lives and are still being formed, adjusted, or confirmed.

As I worked to understand how my experiences and childhood have impacted me, it has been important for me to connect with the foundational aspects that have shaped my movements, decisions, and even my vantage points. Throughout my entrepreneurial career, even as I pushed myself outside my comfort zone, I consistently faced internal resistance and limitations. I struggled to connect with the potential beyond my current capabilities, and these automatic responses and actions kept surfacing.

This drove me deeper into my research and into my desire to understand why I constantly felt pulled back, even as I longed to drive forward. I was on a mission to understand why I was broken, or better yet, why I was programmed not to reach my full potential. The desire to understand the technical aspects of these major elements, like cognitive biases, automaticity, and heuristics, became a passion of mine. My heart was behind this passion, not only to understand how these aspects were affecting me but also to support and assist others in breaking beyond the foundational levels or ceilings they had been programmed to strive toward.

I know some of you will be diving into those technical aspects just like I did, while others are here to understand the process and how to overcome them. I knew I had to work to communicate all of these in a way that was easy to connect with and easy for others to understand. This concept of "lenses" has been the way I've visualized every aspect of my life and every vantage point of who I am. This connection to the disruption of those lenses became the concept of "cracked lenses," a relatable way for me to visualize and explain to others.

You are now aware of my dark secret. I am a bit of a nerd and love pushing into the technical aspects of things for hours at a time. This drive in me is fueled by the desire to be better prepared to work with others and support their growth and progressive development.

Thank you for bearing with me as I walked you through those details, since it is important to understand that the concept of "cracked lenses" isn't just something I made up but is grounded in neuroscientific concepts and backed by extensive research. I wanted to put a more connective concept behind it so people can relate to and understand it better. It is easier to think of a crack in the lens than to try to remember technical terms and research.

For those incredible super-nerds in neuroscience or psychology, just know that this explanation is extremely simplified and focuses on the aspects of these concepts that relate. This is not an extension breakdown, as these concepts are extremely detailed and would take an entire book to do them justice. I encourage people to dive deeper into their own research on them.

Drastic or Not, Cracks Can Form

I feel it is important to clarify something as we move into these concepts. I might give cases or situations that may seem drastic or even extreme to you, but the truth you need to understand is that it doesn't take drastic situations for cracks to form.

The lenses through which we see ourselves can be damaged by many factors throughout our lives. Each one of us has a past that includes situations, circumstances, and even just the way we were raised. The conversations we heard, the things we were told, and how we were treated throughout the years are still affecting how we show up in our lives.

What I find vital to focus on is not so much the fact that you have cracks in your lenses, as we all do, but rather connecting with where they come from and how they are actively affecting the way you see yourself, view your potential, and chase your future.

I have discussed my childhood in many public forums, from stages, podcasts, books, and other groups, and it is important for you to know that my parents are absolutely incredible. I love them and respect them greatly for the examples they have been and the absolute love that they have always shown me. That said, even with the best of parents, cracks form. It took me years to seal up the cracks in my lenses about being an entrepreneur, building wealth, defining what success could look like, and many other aspects of my life because of what I heard and saw and even the advice I was given. All of these things came from a great place in my parents' hearts, as they intended to guide me with their life lessons and the information or knowledge they had at the time.

You and I have to always acknowledge that our parents have their own cracks in their lenses and were raised by people who had cracked lenses as well. Parents, I know you agree with me when I say that you navigate each twist and turn with your best abilities in those moments. I am very open with my son that I am always striving to do the best I can as his father, using all the tools, abilities, and knowledge I have, but I know I will make mistakes. I talk with him about "cracked lenses" and help him become aware of what I say and do that can adjust his perspective.

This is why I want to make sure you understand that even when there isn't a drastic situation in your life, you can still have cracked lenses. I find in my own life, the areas where I don't have trauma, drama, or a major event tied to them are the ones that can affect me even more, as my awareness of them might be a blind spot where a limitation may be located.

One moment in my life I think back to was on a Sunday morning, sitting in a Southern Baptist church when I was about twelve years old. The pastor was pushing hard into the passage found in Matthew 19:24: *"And again I say unto you, It is easier for a camel to go through the eye of a needle, than for a rich man to enter into the kingdom of God"* (KJV).

This didn't cause any major trauma, but I remember thinking to myself that day, and many days afterward, *Man, I do not want to be rich.* In my twelve-year-old mind, I was struggling. If being rich meant I couldn't go to heaven, then there was no way I wanted to be rich. To clarify, I am sure the pastor explained the context about not relying on wealth to earn salvation and the need to rely on God's grace, but my twelve-year-old mind got stuck. I didn't hear anything else after that vivid imagery of a camel trying to fit through the eye of a needle. Knowing that was physically impossible, I mentally connected wealth with not being able to get to heaven. Talk about a mental frame in the back of my mind that only emerged when I was struggling with building and having wealth.

The life we live has so many of these situations, from our past and current ones, engraved on our minds and cracking our lenses from the start of our lives and throughout our lifetimes, even back before we can remember. Dramatic or traumatic situations are not necessary to guide the way you perceive aspects of your life, success, and even your capabilities, abilities, and potential. I've worked with many entrepreneurs and professionals who ended up in a career, industry, or business due to their parents' expectations and the examples they saw growing up.

I don't want you to sit back and blame whatever situation you are currently in on your parents or people from your past, as you have to take ownership of all your actions or lack of actions in your life. However, I do want you to be aware of how and where some of these cracks can form. Have grace for your parents; as I have communicated before, they were raised by imperfect parents themselves.

The one idea to take away from this section is that you need to have an awareness of the fact that cracks can and will be present, no matter your background, upbringing, or experiences. It is important to reflect and identify potential areas of your life that might have been affected.

Relieved, Not a Unicorn

There is an important fact we all have to face: you and I are not unicorns. I know that might come as a shock to you, but it is the truth. What I mean by that is no matter what you have been through or how difficult or complicated your life has been, you are not the only one. I am not saying you are not special, so don't take this the wrong way. I feel that you are built with the opportunity to maximize your uniqueness and make a major impact on this world.

I want you to know that others have faced the same challenges, no matter how horrible they were. I know that the problems we've all faced are not identical. For instance, I have been through a lot of really odd, crazy life experiences and situations. It would be tough to find someone else with exactly the same combination, though many others have gone through very similar aspects and experiences.

To go further, some people have faced the same or similar situations, circumstances, difficulties, hardships, and traumas as you have, and they have been able to grow, develop, achieve greatness, and find major success despite what they have gone through. This is a major reason I have connected with all the people who have joined me in providing the bonus content and resources included with this book. I want you to hear their stories, connect with their struggles, and latch onto the hope that you are not alone and that you can chase a greater life and a better future.

This acknowledgment that you are not a unicorn should bring you peace and hope, diminishing a victim mentality. This is not to minimize anything you have gone through, but rather to help you understand that what has happened in the past does not define your future. Also, this helps you understand that there are others who can support, guide, and encourage you.

I understand that my story and my life, even though they have been filled with major trauma, drama, and difficulties, might not connect directly with or be your exact situation. This doesn't mean I can't help guide you through breaking free from your past and push you to chase after your future with a new lens of who you are and what you are built to take on.

I have worked with many people who have faced major challenges and struggles I have never directly experienced, yet I have helped them overcome their mental obstacles, leverage their strengths, and find success after releasing their holdbacks. Having this experience and opportunity is truly a great privilege. I do not take this lightly, and I am driven to be an impact and guiding light for you and others just like you.

Your story and your life are your own, but you are not alone. That is the most important aspect for you to hold on to at this turning point in your life. There are no such things as unicorns, and I am sorry, even saddened, to tell you that you are not the first, and you will not be the last, to experience the hardships you have faced. I do want you to know that your journey matters, your life has a purpose, and your future is your mission.

Even though others have experienced the same difficulties, hardships, or challenges, you still have a special calling for your life. This is one of the reasons why I wrote this book. As I spent years in pain and endured major hardships, I prayed that God would not let them be in vain. He continues to remind me that it is up to me how I leverage the lessons, growth, and development found only through the battles.

Unicorn or not, I am special, and I know that I have a purpose, and the same is true for you. This is a great time in your life. Whether it is filled with current hardships or you are on the other side recovering, there are lessons you have learned, and will continue to learn, that make you stronger and equip you with unique skill sets. The issue many face is that they allow past issues, hardships, and difficulties to define their future rather than allowing them to be part of their growth, development, and specialized experience, which can be leveraged to achieve greater outcomes.

There is a choice: if you are dedicated to constant improvement and development, the cracks from the past will not break you. The past is a part of your story, but it is not what defines your story.

It's in the Past, So Now What?

What I love about life is the ability to look ahead, to create a future that is entirely your own, a blank canvas waiting for a masterpiece. The past is part of your journey, shaping your experiences and offering lessons you can carry forward. But with that comes a responsibility to ensure that the past does not control you, define you, or derail the future you are capable of building.

Creating the future we desire requires reflection, extracting the lessons, knowledge, and perspectives from our past while intentionally shaping the outcomes we want to see ahead. Let's be honest: there are moments in our past that we absolutely hated. I get it. Some experiences were painful, frustrating, or downright unfair. But here's the reality: you can't change them. What you can change is how much power you continue to give them.

This is where choice comes in. You can allow your past to dictate your next steps, keeping you stuck in old patterns, or you can take control. When you choose to leverage everything you've been through, you unlock the ability to maximize what comes next, armed with a new perspective, a stronger mindset, and a determination to create something greater.

I understand that this is not always easy, and many things from our past tend to haunt us every day: the memories and the things we have heard, seen, and experienced. This is the exact point: we have to change the way we process these things from the past and create a new automatic response that is more focused on where we are going than on where we have been.

These aspects of our past are part of the history of our lives, and there is no way to remove what has happened or how it has molded us. The deciding factor now is what you do with it from here.

I will admit that in my own life, I often allowed the past to control the current moment, and it always left me weakened and unable to show up as the best version of myself. My journey has been marked with many successes, but I still tend to focus on the times I did not show up as I was called to do, and I have allowed the past to dictate how I saw my potential at those times.

Years ago, I had to take control of how I viewed myself, my day, my opportunities, and my actions. I had to constantly work on the frame in which I viewed my past, my hardships, and those traumatic experiences that haunted my self-security. Those voices from the past and those memories and limitations imposed on my life by others created nagging mindsets. I had to learn to reframe and remove power from them.

Breaking free from these anchors from your past and chasing after the hope of the future you have in front of you is what you should be fully focused on. As you work through the pages in this book, it is important to do the required reflection and take ownership of this part of your journey.

You are never stuck in the past unless you allow yourself to be. The daunting uphill battle facing you as you work through this process may leave you with great anxiety or even bring you to shut down, but working through the past and recognizing that it does not define the rest of your life brings hope and encouragement.

Cracked but Overcame

I understand that when you are in the midst of the struggle, dealing with the daily fight and feeling that you are one second away from drowning, it is seemingly impossible to have any glimpse of hope. The perspective you need to maintain when you are in the storm is one of the most difficult battles you will fight, especially when you allow comparisons and the glorified pedestals of others to creep in.

Our society has allowed people to use "glory reels" to create false depictions of their lives, leading some to feel a sense of failure, inadequacy, and even hopelessness. This is why I found it important to include interviews in the resources section from people who have gone through challenging situations, diving into their lives and the hardships they have faced. Their lives and what they have overcome are presented in a way that encourages you to know you are not alone. The truth is that each one of us has to face a life that is messy, and not any one of us is exempt from the hurt, pain, and mental struggles that come. Everyone interviewed is incredibly supportive of this book and excited to participate in this project to support you on your journey.

I know that when I am sitting in my darkest moments, I have to identify hope to cling to, and that hope is found in knowing that others have worked through similar hard times and not only survived but thrived on the other side. I know that each of you reading this is in a different phase of your journey. The interviews presented here are from people who have joined me in making an impact on your life, and they are great, shining lights dedicated to showing up for those in the midst of their darkest moments. Don't miss out on this opportunity to connect to the stories of others and give yourself hope for the next phase of your journey.

Some people can't stand the thought of moving to the bonus sections of a book until they have read the book completely, but don't let yourself get discouraged. Dive into these interviews to gather fuel for your journey and learn from people who have been through loss, abuse of all types, suicide attempts, physical devastation, emotional neglect, and abandonment but overcame their situations to pursue greatness and achieve remarkable accomplishments.

My good friend Amberly Lago had a dream of being a professional dancer and left her small town in Texas to drive to Los Angeles to pursue it. She was confronted with the reality of what this new town brought the day she was mugged shortly after moving. The voices in her head from back home rang loudly, *You are crazy*, yet her determination to push harder and dive full force into this pursuit was relentless.

Amberly expressed, "I've had naysayers my entire life, and I have learned that I want to prove to myself that I can do something." This mindset and dedicated focus were leveraged to get her through this tough time, landing her great opportunities and outcomes during this phase of her life. Although she continued to have hardships and what others would call impossible circumstances, she would not allow herself to be broken.

Now, if you are able to spend even a moment with Amberly, you will feel her dedication to bringing joy to everyone she comes into contact with. In the bonus resource, you can listen to her heart and the lengthy list of hardships she has faced, as well as her encouragement for your journey.

For ease of access, I found it important to include this QR code to access the interviews and resources.

Leverage or Let Limit

A choice must be made, and you might be facing it at this exact moment. Will you push forward and leverage your experiences, or let them limit your potential by leaving them unaddressed?

You might feel that you are better than those who came before you and believe you can muscle your way to success. I will tell you that having that drive is incredibly important and will build momentum, but if you don't address the cracked lenses that can derail your progress, you could find yourself limited, derailed, or stuck in cycles of insanity on your journey. Remember, no one is exempt from these holdbacks. In my life, the unaddressed issues always seemed to come up at the worst moments, derailing major steps toward my "lighthouse."

I know that, for many, it isn't popular to dig into past pain and the hardships that you once dealt with, but the future you are capable of reaching requires hard work. This will be tough, and from my personal experience, it creates many feelings, turmoil, and even restless nights. However, hard work is what produces the greatest version of you.

If you run from difficulties and seek comfort instead of progress and development, your life will reflect the easy paths rather than the right ones. Consider the long-term potential of your life and connect to the fact that the hard work today could be what allows a greater tomorrow than you could ever imagine.

After working with many entrepreneurs, coaches, consultants, and business owners, I have found a common theme: those who are willing to do the hard work are better able to leverage their past to maximize their potential. I have faith that God can redeem us and help us leverage even the most challenging moments, seasons, and circumstances. In my life, though the circumstances were extremely difficult and just plain heartbreaking, God has used them to help me gain perspective, build my endurance, learn resilience, and be more compassionate toward others.

I know that if the hardships layered throughout my past hadn't happened, I wouldn't have been able or willing to write this book. The difficulties I have faced have given me an endless supply of drive and ambition, not to find success but to leave a legacy of impact for the people I can reach. I am dedicated to helping others find hope and encouragement through their hard times.

This is why you have to decide whether to let the hardships and difficulties you face limit your future and potential or leverage them to maximize the life you have in front of you. The past can never be changed; it is the story that has been written up to this moment, but what you do with it is within your control. The life ahead is what you get to manage, and if you are anything like me, you don't want to let your past dictate how your life turns out. You have to take ownership of each step of this journey and set a foundation of growth that starts today.

Your Message to You

Your life will never be greater than what you accept and expect from yourself. I can lay out incredible concepts in an organized fashion and deliver detailed action steps to you on a silver platter, but until you are ready for change and determined to create a greater life for yourself, no one can give you enough guidance. Those who are hungry and driven to progress seek the right advice, direction, and action steps.

I trust that, as you continue to move forward in this book and on your journey, you will be a person of action. If you are, I promise this book will give you insight, direction, and focused movements to take with you. The message you need to communicate to yourself is that this point is a catalyst for making the decision to be dedicated to providing a better life for the future you. The sacrifices you make today will be part of the story you are writing and the legacy you leave behind.

In this moment, there is a need to adjust your perspective and gain new insight into aspects of your life, experiences, and upbringing to tease out the areas that are negatively impacting the momentum you are capable of building. Remember, it isn't only drastic or extreme situations in your life that have a major impact on how you see yourself, your potential, and your capabilities, and even on the decisions you make about your career, finances, relationships, and other areas of your life. You have to cut out the noise in your life and truly focus on who you are, what you are capable of achieving, and what the greatest version of you could ever be.

This might require you to disconnect from social media or other environments where people are more focused on their glory reels than on being open about their true lives, struggles, and hardships. There is no room for comparison and false realities in your headspace. You have to dedicate yourself to self-reflection and internal work, and you cannot afford to be compromised by these outside factors that, in most cases, are based upon fallacies rather than truths.

What would it look like for you to step back, embrace the present, remain receptive to truth, and be prepared to embrace your true self? Be open and honest about all that you have been through: the great things, the hard things, the failures, and the successes. Are you ready to accept it all as a part of your story? Are you prepared to confront those areas where you have fallen short? Are you ready to accept the fact that you have a skill set and capabilities that, if applied properly, could be leveraged to reach greater success than what you have allowed yourself to settle for?

Some of you are sitting in this moment more prepared to write a dissertation about all your shortfalls and weaknesses than you are to willingly accept your countless strengths. Others are looking at these questions and have a false reality of how great they really are; they have ignored their shortcomings and failures. The only things that matter are truth, honesty, openness, reflection, and the willingness to push deeper into who you are to reach the greater future you are capable of achieving.

The story of your life is yours to write. In my own life, my past can be hard to face at times, but the ability to work with others and impact lives by walking them through the principles I have learned on my journey makes it all worth it.

As you close out this chapter, take time to reflect, cut out the noise, and fully dedicate yourself to growth, development, and uncovering those areas of holdbacks that could be haunting your progress. The dreams you are striving for, or once held firm to, cannot be broken or forgotten because of a lack of awareness or unwillingness to dive deep and push hard. Have a serious conversation with yourself about where you are in this moment and whether you are ready to confront every aspect of who you are, your mindsets, and the cracked lenses that could be destructive to your future.

CHAPTER 2

The Dreams

Sitting in the park, I watched my six-year-old son run around with his friends. They were not focused on the surrounding distractions of cars passing by, overflowing garbage cans, pizza boxes being blown around, or even the crying babies. These boys were locked into their imagination and the storyline they were living in at that moment. The battle they were fighting and the destruction they were preventing were the only things that mattered.

I watched as all of them fought for their lives against an imaginary group of evil warriors, captured them, and then celebrated when they overcame the darkness. I saw their exaggerated movements, which I am sure looked completely different in their heads, and I laughed as they all argued about who would face the next monster, as if there could only be one hero at a time inside the enactment. They pushed past their slight bickering to take on a monster that had grown into an impossible adversary for just one of them and required the entire group.

They were deep in the scuffle when, through all the battle sounds and imaginary near-death experiences, a loud, disrupting tone from a woman nearby blew like a train horn: "Just stop! You are being too loud. We can't have any conversations with how loud you boys are being." She continued on and on in an extremely rude, opinionated tone, correcting their "unacceptable" behavior. This person decided it was her right to go over to this group of about ten boys and tell them to stop playing. (To make matters even worse, she allowed the monster to get away.)

For those of you who know me, I am sure you could guess that this didn't go over well with me. I approached the situation with as much patience and curiosity as possible and asked the woman which of the boys was her child. She told me none of them were. I continued to communicate to her, on behalf of all the boys' parents, as kindly as possible, that she needed to refrain from addressing our children, as her actions were a complete disruption to the entire experience at the park.

I feel it is important to let you know that this was a large park with about five playgrounds and countless benches that she and her friends could have relocated to for a peaceful conversation. I understand conversations are important, but a park is a place for children to be free to enjoy themselves and let out all their energy for a smoother evening, particularly for us parents with more hyperactive kids. To not bore you with all the details of this conversation, I will just say it didn't go great, but in the end, the other boys' parents joined in, and the woman was clearly no longer welcome at this playground.

After this, the boys were able to rebuild the scene destroyed by the "joy killer" and get back to fighting the monster. In less than five minutes, the group of boys gave up on their quest, and the fun was over. The actions of one person dismantled the excitement and momentum of overcoming darkness and protecting what was good. All of these kids went from being heroes on a mission to being messy, thirsty, hungry, and defeated. Their dreams of overcoming the monster and becoming heroes no longer mattered, as they were brought back to the harsh reality that some monsters couldn't be fought or overcome.

In the conversations that followed with my son, I encouraged him not to let one person's actions dictate how he shows up. I remember trying to give him a motivational talk, or at least one for a six-year-old, explaining how some people cannot stand it when others are living in joy and happiness, and that the only thing we can do is control our actions and how we respond.

The most frustrating thing for me is that nothing I said seemed to lift this dark cloud that had come over the kids. I know that in the scope of life, this is just a small circumstance. A few days later, he could have easily remembered just the killer battle that he had with his friends. But after that day, their battles were different whenever he and those kids went to the park. Their excitement diminished, and the joy that occurred was never duplicated. This one circumstance had created programming that, if they really allowed themselves to get fully engulfed in their dreams, the evil monster that could not be fought would come back and ruin their fun again.

I know you are not living in a fantasy world with monsters and don't have hopes of slaying dragons and saving a princess from a tower, or at least, I hope not. Instead, you are facing reality, a life that you are actually living out day after day. And you may be facing joy-killing experiences. At times, you may even feel like you are being crushed by the weight of the requirements that are put upon you. I have heard some of the most heart-wrenching stories about the burdens that people have had to bear.

I do not want you to feel that I am comparing your life to a group of boys living in their imaginations at a park, but this story has an important lesson I want you to connect with. I want you to see how one person's actions in a particular circumstance of your life can change your programming. Yes, maybe this lady isn't always this awful, but in that moment, her inability to look beyond her own wants and conveniences instilled programming in others that shouldn't have been.

Your life is filled with these programming moments, and let's be real, even the best parents out there create some messed-up programming inside their children. I, for one, have had to tell my kids that I am not perfect. I am trying to navigate the parenting waters as best I can and have needed to apologize a lot along the way. We will dig into the programming issues a bit more in the book, but right now, I want to focus on your dreams.

What are dreams? Even though it doesn't feel right to give you a "definition" of what a dream is, as it can mean many things, I still want to walk you through how I perceive dreams and how I have seen them in my own and clients' lives, in many variations. The simple idea of being able to imagine or see a greater moment than the one you are currently living in or experiencing can easily help define what a dream is.

I do want to go deeper into this and even dive into the ability to see your life beyond your current restraints, circumstances, and limitations, which could lay the groundwork for dreaming. I see dreaming as the ability to envision life beyond your current capabilities, goals beyond what you can currently achieve, and a future that cannot be attained given the exact skill sets, abilities, knowledge, and resources you currently possess. Approaching the concept of dreams from this angle provides multiple levers to adjust, expand, and forecast as you consider the long-term potential of your compounding growth and development. Then you can leverage that understanding to develop your capabilities to the maximum.

As I have said, these are just the ways I consider dreams, a practical way I have been able to identify the gateway to dreaming greater. The great part about this is that you do not need to connect to an exact definition of a dream or dreaming.

I want to take you through a brief understanding of how I look at dreams to make sure you understand I am not talking about chasing unicorns or slaying dragons. Those sound like a fun time, but I do not want to waste my time or yours discussing things that are not achievable. I want to focus on the three types of dreams that are important for you to connect to in this process. Then we can continue to build on this concept.

The Dreams You Cannot Allow to Be Broken

The first dream type is the easiest for us to connect with; these are your goals, ambitions, and hopes for the future. This might seem obvious, but many individuals are in the process of letting their dreams fall by the wayside because they've stopped connecting to them.

This is where I want you to take the time to go back and connect with all the details in the dreams you are currently chasing. Some of you might have vision boards; others may have financial goals, relational goals, business goals, and even goals related to how you want to be viewed by those around you. Too many of us are not honest with others or ourselves about the true elements of our dreams. Some of what we want or hope for might feel a little wrong at times, but I need you to connect to and really understand that they need to be identified. The different aspects of our lives should all have dreams associated with them.

I feel it is important for you to take a few minutes and really connect to the dreams you are chasing. I am not talking about setting global goals, but rather about digging deeper into the more specific aspects of your dreams and connecting to the why behind each one. It is so easy to set goals and outcomes as the guideposts for what we are chasing, but the truth is that we have to emotionally connect with what we are pushing to accomplish.

I find that financial goals don't really motivate me directly, and the real purpose behind seeking them is the freedom that I have always dreamed of. The freedom to have time flexibility allows me to be more present with my family and to maximize my relationships. The ability to achieve financial freedom gives my family the experiences I was unable to have growing up in a lower-income household. I want to be part of supporting my parents, as they were such an incredible support to me during my childhood and throughout my life. I want to experience new places and have the flexibility and financial means to enjoy travel.

These dreams have kept me motivated for almost twenty years as an entrepreneur. With the financial freedom I gained in 2024 from the sale of my flagship company and my other companies, I have found that my dreams go far beyond the freedom of time and the relationships in my life. I have uncovered massive dreams rooted in my potential to impact lives and to leverage the hardships and struggles I encountered on my journey to encourage others.

I know I have the ability, through openness and vulnerability, to dive deep into aspects of my journey that are not sexy or glamorous but are the realities that many entrepreneurs and other individuals face. The dreams of my life have been an ever-changing adventure, never something set in stone. This is all laid out here so you know that just because something was your dream years ago doesn't mean it needs to be the current focus.

Early on in this book and process, I want you to lock in on your dreams. You must connect to them and make sure they are detailed and explicit, not just vague, undefined statements like "I want to be wealthy and successful," but put definitions behind all of them.

Lay out all of your dreams and ask yourself "why" for each of them. Don't allow yourself to be safe and timid about how far out you set your dreams and the level at which you create them. It is important to get excited and feel connected to the potential outcomes of the dreams you lay out. Detail them, and then begin connecting with them daily, using them as part of the fuel that drives you to greater action.

These are dreams you cannot allow to be broken. The road you will travel as you continue to move forward will either have results and successes that constantly elevate you toward the dreams you are chasing, or they will be a part of the regrets that haunt you as you lick your wounds if you allow your own self-destructive tendencies to win. These types of dreams are our current ones; they are the most tangible, encouraging us to take new or greater action.

For any of you who know me, whether directly or indirectly, I am sure you are aware that I will challenge you on these later in this book. For now, you can lock these in, knowing that I will help you expand on them. It may get uncomfortable, but that is where growth comes from. I am not here as a cheerleader in your life but rather to challenge you, guide you, and help you achieve a greater life for yourself.

The Dreams You Once Knew

The second type of dream can be an area of profound regret: dreams that are a solemn reminder of who we hoped we would become and, to others, of the death of our potential. This type of dream is the one you once knew. I am not talking about childish dreams, like those of my son and his friends at the park, ones that lack any foundation or realistic reach. To make sure I am fully clear, I am also not talking about discounting dreams that, because of your choices, are now less likely to be realized.

These dreams are layered with goals, ambitions, and aspects of our lives as we move into adulthood, allowing us to see the future with fewer jaded restrictions. These dreams came to us before we faced disheartening realities regarding the level of resistance we would encounter. Those dreams from the past may also have had some unrealistic features to them, but the heart of those dreams was at the core of who you are.

Too many people lose sight of the vision, mission, hopes, and better lives that they once dreamed of. These dreams from our past might have been easy to walk away from, assuming they were created by a false reality we could not live in.

My dreams of becoming a cop, having an impact on people, and serving others were confronted with the harsh reality of what the job actually entailed. The realization that the general public didn't always see cops as people they could trust, count on, or even be seen with made living out aspects of this dream extremely difficult at times. This, coupled with the politics, trauma, and even straight-up evil that I was required to confront as a police officer, gave room for what felt like a slow death of my original dreams of impact and service.

Then, to make matters even worse, the reality of that career being stripped from me due to medical issues left me with scrambled eggs of those dreams. Even in this situation, there were still core fundamentals of these dreams that I could never let die. The fact that I had a deep desire to impact and serve held true at the root of everything I did in my businesses and all my ventures. Yes, the first dream, you may say, became broken, but I would argue that it just took a new form as I adapted and adjusted my career.

This is only one of my early dreams that has been adapted into a theme throughout my life despite adverse circumstances. I could list many dreams that, during a particular season of my life, I lost focus on and even gave up on. I thank God that He continued to remind me of those dreams I let go of for a while. I had to dig deep into the foundations of each dream and work to rebuild them to ensure I never lost sight of them again.

It is so easy in our lives to excuse the release of dreams from our past, and let's face it, society even drives us to fit into specific boxes or live up to certain expectations. Often, these go against our natural bent and our need for freedom, unorthodox structures, and gateways to a greater future. This is why I want to take a moment to help you connect to the dreams you once knew and identify why you let them die.

Why did you allow your life to get so off track from the goals you once set? I know there are many aspects to this, including people in your life who influenced the derailment of your dreams. The foundation of all the cracked lenses you use in your decision-making can be a major factor, but it should never excuse you from walking away from your dreams.

I have met people with what I would consider limitless potential, but they have allowed their lives to be contained, safe, and secure rather than exercising their full potential. They have let external factors take over and destroy their early-life dreams, leaving them with regrets, failures, and a list of "what ifs." This is a huge part of why I wrote this book. I want to address these factors and help you revisit your goals and chase your dreams again, with a stronger foundation and tools at your disposal to get you refocused.

As you can probably gather by the way I am laying this out, I am rather passionate about the dreams from your past. There is a reason you had them. The goals you set, the ambitions you defined, and the purpose you identified in your past were never meant to be abandoned or forgotten.

What are those things in your life? What were those burning desires that drove you years ago? What hopes for impact drove you before you felt the burden of the financial cost of life? What were the ambitions that you wanted to pursue before the baseball bat of reality hit you in the face? These dreams from your past, of the ones you once knew, cannot stay forgotten. Some aspects must remain, while others may need to be adapted, adjusted, and perfected.

The life you are living now has so much potential, and the future that you can create can be incredible. I understand there are aspects of your past—the hurt, trauma, and hardships—that put what feels like an endless weight on your shoulders. These setbacks create significant resistance to taking the next step forward. Yes, the past contains many unwanted experiences for each of us. You must lay a core foundation, a true connection to the reasons behind each dream you once had. What are the aspects and principles behind each of your past dreams?

To those who are currently in the midst of hardship or traumatic circumstances, I want to offer you a quick word of encouragement. When your goals and ambitions are anchored in purpose, the hardest moments lose their power because your focus is fixed on your "lighthouse"—your focus on something greater than the present moment. I know in my life, the more difficult things I encounter, the more abilities I gain to accomplish my goals. Hard times foster significant growth, and enduring life's challenges is the only way to develop resilience.

These dreams from your past, the dreams you once knew, must be rejuvenated, and core aspects must be extrapolated from them. This might require you to refresh past dreams and even set new goals related to each one's purpose, vision, or principles.

What you cannot do is allow the dreams to die, no matter the demands of life that are in front of you. You cannot allow them to be broken because of what life has brought you. This cannot be the end of the dreams you once knew; they were not instilled inside of you just to be set aside and become a gateway to regrets.

The Dreams You Never Knew Could be Yours

This third type of dream haunts me almost endlessly: the dreams we never knew could be ours. What are the greater goals that you could set and achieve if you knew you could compound results and defy any limitations that were instilled in you? Why did past generations who came before you and me limit the capabilities of the family, group, demographic, or even the culture as a whole?

Why do we sit inside the false limitations in front of us? This may be frustrating to think about. I could give you countless examples of parents who tell their children things like, "In our family, we are talented with our hands and are meant to use them. Our family isn't built for college." Or "I am the 4th generation attorney or doctor, and you will make the 5th generation." Then there are the families that make plans for family business succession, where weight is put on children to continue a business that has been family-owned for generations. "This business has been in our family since my granddaddy's granddaddy started it."

Many families place expectations on their kids about which schools to attend and which careers are prestigious enough. But where are those parents considering the greatest strengths and capabilities of their children? What about the dreams that children are built to create for themselves, even greater ones than their parents could achieve?

I know that some of you have heard my story. I will make sure to give my parents great respect and love, as they have been incredible in so many ways. My father is the best example of a hardworking, family-oriented leader. He balances a relentless, hard-charging leadership style with a dedication to providing his loved ones with a better life. My mother is the kindest and most caring person you could ever meet. She would give away everything to help those in need.

These two, and their incredible leadership and example, gave me the ability to break through the mold that was set in place. This mold was not out of a desire to hold me back but rather as a form of protection and guidance to help me find what they considered financial security. I am so appreciative of who they are and the heart of everything they taught me.

Even so, I felt there were major limitations for what I could hope to achieve in life. I had programming that set expectations, not for the type of career to chase after but for the financial security behind those career choices. Jobs that had retirement and pension options were a high priority, an idea instilled in me from a young age. I also had tremendous respect for financial management, as my father somehow provided for us four kids and my mother on a single income for the majority of our childhood. He was a master at penny-pinching and negotiating with us kids to take faster showers and keep the lights off. To this day, Taco Bell bean burritos have a special place in my heart. We were bribed as kids to help lower the power and water bill, and part of the savings was used to reward us with these magical burritos and soft tacos.

These and other early lessons came from a great place in my parents' hearts. However, these lessons didn't give me the entire foundation to chase my dreams or fully prepare me to create the best life I was capable of. There were many days on my journey when I felt guilty about having an abundance of financial resources. I felt something was wrong with building wealth. I also had to break away from the idea of needing a retirement or pension within a career. I felt like I was programmed to live a life without financial freedom, to work until I was 65, and then have a limited retirement, rather than live in abundance. This had to be disconnected from me so I could drive hard at the entrepreneurial vision I had for myself after law enforcement.

It's important to realize that parents have their own programming and cracked lenses that they raise us in, which expanded into the groups you were involved with, such as church groups, the Boy or Girl Scouts, the culture you were raised in, and other demographics that defined who you were and were expected to be. These create a death of dreaming, as the future before us often feels already defined. We are walking a road laid by someone else, and as long as we stay on it, it is accepted. If we detour toward our own mission, vision, or dream, it can create disruption and disapproving responses that may not be easy for many of us to endure.

These are all things we have to challenge in our dreams, goal-setting, ambition-driven pursuits, and future-chasing. You cannot allow the cracked lenses and programming of your past to dictate how your future will end up. You are capable of so much more than you could ever imagine at this moment. I have achieved things that the younger version of me would have found mind-blowing. I could never have had these types of dreams when I was in my early twenties. My mind had so many limitations laced throughout and restrictions instilled inside.

However, I can tell you that I have been where you are currently, and I even feel in this moment, writing these words, that I still have so much more work to do to allow myself to see the full vision of capabilities that are inside of me. I drive forward every day, challenging what I know, what I feel, what I think, and even the dreams I have laid for myself. The goals that I set must scare me, and the goals that I implement must be beyond anything I feel I can achieve.

Even this, while giving me great growth and expanding what I have accomplished, remains a limited version of what I could achieve. I have jokingly told people that I set "Depend goals," meaning that they make me want to put on a pair of Depends just by setting them. I require my ambitions to be far beyond anything I feel I can accomplish with who I am today. I know the goals I set for myself require me to be dedicated to growth and development and to never let my cracked lenses, fears, and insecurities win.

The stakes for your future are too high to settle for a vision blurred by cracked lenses. Becoming aware of these distortions and their historical grip on your life is the only way to stop your past from sabotaging your legacy. You have to tap into the dreams that you never knew could be yours. You have to break the mold, free yourself from expectations, and chase after a future that scares you to even think about. To me, this third type of dream is the hardest to swallow and the most impactful to discuss with people on this journey.

You cannot fill your future with the dreams you were built for if you are still viewing your potential through the narrow, cracked lenses of your past. Your capabilities aren't the problem; the limitations you've allowed to dictate your direction are.

Circumventing Future Regrets

Understanding more about types of dreams and reading passionate explanations about them isn't going to be all that is required for you to have a major life change and take on the world. The purpose of all of this is for you to hear and connect with your dreams, and by doing so, you can never remove that awareness. I want this to be something that haunts you, challenges you, and even unsettles you. That might not be what you want, but many times, change doesn't happen overnight; it requires a belief to be challenged, a fundamental aspect to be shaken, or something that previously felt finite to become infinite.

This is not the end, but just the beginning of a new way to chase your future and create new dreams for yourself. I would say I am sorry about the hard work you will have to dedicate yourself to, but I cannot. I wish someone had challenged me every step of my journey with what I believed I was capable of and how I viewed my potential for a greater life. It took me years of fighting the limitations instilled in me from a young age, along with other ongoing experiences that dynamically shaped how I viewed myself and what I could take on in life. If I hadn't pushed myself to think differently and challenge all that I knew, these holdbacks could have crippled not just what I could achieve but also the people I could reach and impact.

The regrets that keep you awake at night will not only be failures that you could have corrected but also the achievements you didn't know you could have chased after and accomplished. I am not here to cast judgment or tell you that I have it all figured out. Rather, I have figured out that I do not yet know everything I am capable of achieving, and I want to push myself to greatness beyond what I can imagine.

Some see this restlessness as a curse, but I see it as endless potential that I must create. This requires me to push beyond comfort and the core facets that are so easy to use as excuses when they are all I have known. Understanding these dreams and connecting with each of them pushes me to never allow them to become broken. I move forward knowing I am a work in progress and acknowledging that certain limiting beliefs I carry can throttle the full expression of what I am capable of becoming. I have to put the checks and balances in place to make sure I am not taking actions that could derail my momentum.

How are you going to reflect on your dreams differently now that you have this new awareness of the different dream types? If this chapter didn't resonate with you or cause you to pause, I would be deeply concerned. This chapter about dreams is a core, fundamental aspect of your desire for a greater future. I hope you take the time to challenge the way you dream, the goals you set, and the potential you see in the results of your future actions.

What I don't want is for you to walk away from this chapter with any form of judgment or to beat yourself up for not having pushed yourself to your potential. That is why I want to be open about my own life. We are all works in progress, and we need to continually push ourselves to think, act, and even dream differently. The dreams of your future must be challenged, and the best version of yourself requires extreme growth, even in the way that you allow yourself to dream.

CHAPTER 3

Challenge Your Dreams

The questions lined the page, and I focused on each aspect, but they all started with "what if." The focused and reflective process that I'd started seemed to keep my mind stuck in a cycle of questioning the "why" behind my circumstances and left me with simple questions that challenged my reality:

What if I set my goals higher than I can even imagine?

What if I built something that could be sold for more money than I ever thought I would be able to accumulate?

What if I stopped letting the limitations drive my decision-making and allowed some wonder and unknowns to be a part of my future planning?

What if I forced myself to get uncomfortable with what I challenged myself to take on?

These were among the many questions I pushed myself to dive deeper into, and countless others were part of my planning during my third year of business. None of these were easy questions to answer, and many of them gave me great heartburn. I had just made it through the phase of business where I felt the entire world was crumbling every week and feared the dismantling and destruction of what I was building at every turn.

For this year of business, I chose the theme "The Year of the Beyond" in hopes of thriving toward a future goal rather than just surviving the storms of business. At this point, I had made it through two very tough years with many struggles, but I didn't want to keep fighting the same old battles. I had to focus my vision beyond those hardships. Each day, I felt as though I were in a fight for my financial life rather than setting goals and achieving non-survival-related ambitions. I had been through some very dark financial days, even to the point where, in my first full year of business, I lost my house. This was one of the most humbling experiences and a massive kick to my pride.

Many people minimize the challenges of starting a business and feel they can take on whatever comes their way. I was one of them. I felt I had the entire plan all dialed in and ready to go, but I had underestimated the rough economic climate of 2008 and 2009. Of course, it is a great time to start a business right in the middle of a major recession; everyone knows this. Keep in mind, I had already overcome paralysis and was still facing a journey of uphill battles with my heart condition. I wondered if the medical trauma I'd endured made me feel like, no matter what happened in the business, it couldn't be as bad as what I had faced medically and as a police officer.

I will be honest: I was gravely naïve when I launched my business, and losing my house was a massive wake-up call. This pushed me deep into planning and theming every year, based on the development I needed to grow as an entrepreneur.

In this third year of business, I had to go beyond survival mode and really connect with what I wanted my business to become. What did I want this mysterious word, "success," to look like in my life? How did I want to leverage my business to be a part of the greater vision for my life, my family, and my future? These are all the questions that required me to look at everything from a "What if?" perspective.

So, I dove headfirst into the entire planning process, with every question starting with "What if." Pushing myself to think outside the box, I had to confront all the limitations that my head constantly wanted to impose. This year was exactly what I needed, challenging myself to think beyond and set tremendously ambitious goals. Overcoming the fears created by just setting these goals felt almost impossible.

I went through this process relentlessly and had to face a lot of limitations that had been programmed inside of me. I shook up my beliefs about my capabilities and challenged aspects of my childhood that left me feeling pulled in different directions. What if I challenged the core fundamentals of everything I believed about what life should look like and what I was capable of going after and achieving? I left no rocks unturned; I pushed deep with a self-reflective tool I have now, named "the inner two-year-old," which questions the "why" behind everything. I would keep asking myself the "why" behind every limitation and belief about myself, my future, my opportunities, and my potential success.

For me, this was the only way to push beyond survival or a limited definition of success. I had to go deep into the weeds to figure out who I was, what I was capable of achieving, why I was pushing so hard, and what I would be satisfied with. This year of focusing on "the beyond" was one of the hardest years of growth in terms of my perspectives, belief systems, and cognitive processes, but the work paid off.

The goal-setting, dream-chasing, and unlocking a new level of resilience gave me unmatched drive and ambition. I was setting goals and dreaming in ways that seemed borderline insane to me at that time, but I was not afraid to push toward them. I knew that even if I didn't reach those goals and dreams, I would definitely be closer than if I had never set them in motion.

The one thing I want to make sure I bring full circle for you is that I achieved all the goals I set for myself and my business during that year, and I did it all in less time than I had set for myself. I am not telling you this to brag, but rather the opposite: look how limited my goal-setting and dream-casting were in my third year of business. Even in the year of the beyond, when I was supposed to be setting goals with unlimited potential, I achieved them within the next seven years. Those goals felt like an impossibility within a twenty- to thirty-year business run, but I accomplished them all in under a third of the time. Although I didn't get to the full extent of the beyond here, I will attest it was the year I had the catalyst that allowed me to challenge my thinking, goals, and dreams forever.

This is where I would love for you to meet me: a place of willingness to challenge your thinking, goals, and dreams. After simplifying the different dream types, I hope you have taken the need to focus on and reflect on your dreams seriously. I don't believe you should move past something that is a pillar in your foundation and required for your greatest outcome in life.

Now, I know that some of you are thinking, *Nate, let's move past the dreams and into the nuggets of wisdom.* If that is you, then what I will tell you is that if you don't take the nuggets in the prior chapter and this one seriously, you will miss out on the potential greatness of what your life could look like. It would be like going through Chick-fil-A and ordering your nuggets and favorite sauces, only to realize, as you pull into your house to enjoy the nuggies, that you left them behind.

Challenging your dreams is vital. Challenging your goals and questioning your ambitions are fundamental points of growth. I am the one tasked with bringing the heat, and I do this only out of love for you and the future I know you can achieve, the setbacks you can break free from, and your ability to create an entirely new vision for yourself.

This is a great point in your life to stop accepting what you know, stop living in the same cycle, and process without questioning the "why" behind it. This is also the point at which you need to ask yourself the "What if" questions.

I want you to start with one of the most important of them all: *What if I stepped back, questioned every aspect of my life, and challenged myself to create a greater life than I could ever imagine? What are the dreams that I could have for my life?*

Don't get sidetracked here. I am not talking about questioning your marriage or responsibilities as a parent, but rather the mental programming, expectations, and pressures that keep you from taking different actions. These may also be the limitations in the way you see yourself, your future, your opportunities, and your capabilities.

Serious in the Midst of Dreaming

As you connect to the dreams in your life, it's crucial to challenge each one of them. This applies to your goals, hopes, and ambitions, as well as your vision of the purpose for your future. You also have to pay close attention to what has held back so many others who have come before you from setting their greatest goals, achieving their full potential, or reaching their greatness. It's not just about being driven or hungry enough to pursue your future; it's also about knowing how you can be derailed.

An unrealized major problem for many people is that they have default cognitive processes that can create significant setbacks and even lead to failure. These same cognitive processes kept me from setting the real goals and ambitions I was capable of pursuing. That is why, early on in this book, I find it important to include a quick self-check: it doesn't matter what stage of your success journey you are on; there is a major silent success killer you need to be aware of.

We each have these mental holdbacks and programming. We need to put in very specific effort to make sure these things are acknowledged and held accountable so they do not hold us captive. The future in front of you should be driven by your hopes and dreams and confirmed by your efforts, actions, and dedicated steps toward success. This moment in your life should be one of reflection, a time to ensure you are taking the necessary actions and eliminating any potential distractions or derailers that keep you from pursuing and challenging your dreams.

At this moment, you might not understand why I would introduce this point of tension in a chapter that is supposed to be all about your dreams, but my focus is to help you succeed and equip you to challenge your dreams. I am passionate about never allowing holdbacks and derailers to keep us from achieving our dreams, especially those we can identify and get ahead of.

I strongly advise you to examine any cycles and broken fundamentals in your life. How have you reacted in the different situations that you have encountered? How have you handled adversity in the different areas of your life? When difficulties threaten the results of your action steps, how do you adapt? What are the feelings that drive your actions, whether good or bad? What is your internal programming that could create an issue in your success journey? What have you seen others do that could change how you act in similar situations? What areas from your childhood might have created cracked lenses that affect how you see yourself, your future, your potential, and your dreams? What areas are affecting the full development of the dream casting that you are currently in the midst of?

Freedom in Your Dreaming

For some people, dreaming might come naturally; they might have the ability to see unlimited potential in front of them. Traditionally, these are the visionaries who have dreams for days. I love spending time with these people, but because of the way my brain works, I have trouble living in the clouds with them for long. I feel that the way I am built requires my dreams to be connected to a realistic, attainable goal or to see the gear wheels connect to make them a reality.

I realize that I create my own handicap when I live in this way. I struggle with unrestricted hope and ambition, but I love imagining the possibilities of connecting unlimited parts to achieve outcomes that may seem impossible to others. This is how I establish the groundwork for reaching new heights. Some of you are just like me, what I call limited visionaries. We can cast a future goal, ambition, and vision, but we need a grounded foundation and connectors that allow us to fully have ownership of them.

I am not saying that being built like I am is any better than those who are visionaries, as they also have great potential and incredible strengths. Of course, there are some who might struggle to set goals beyond the next step or others who are gifted at executing the steps of someone else's vision. Each of us has to be real about our giftings, but in any of these cases, they should not hold us back from creating our *own* dream. The dreams you set might lack the full ambitions of a visionary or your ability to understand the process that will be required, but you should always focus on driving toward a greater future.

The honesty that we all have to face when we are working through challenges and creating the greatest dreams for our lives is what drives and motivates us to a greater future. You don't have to be a visionary to recognize that you want to create a better life for your kids. It doesn't take an out-of-the-box thinker to know you don't want to work until you're sixty-five.

What if you allowed yourself to dream about all the people you could help if you took a risk and started a business, providing jobs, financial security, and opportunities to support charities? You might not have the vision for the exact avenue to get there, but creating the details for a better life and defining it are part of the dream.

As I mentioned, I am driven by freedom. My dreams include different freedoms for different reasons. They no longer include a specific business operational outcome but instead freedom and what that could mean for the people I reach and impact. That's why I don't want you to focus on your personality type or the skills you use to plan right now. Instead, I want you to dive deeply into the passions, purpose, driving forces, fuel, and other aspects that push you to want a better life.

If you are a visionary, hybrid, or other type and can see a specific business direction as part of your dream, feel free to incorporate it into what you are striving for. The most important part is to get outside of the here and now and force yourself to think beyond your comfort zone.

I want you to understand that there is not one specific layout or design for what someone's dreams should look like. Some people dream of living on the beach and smoking cigars every day. But that has never been a driver for me, and to put it plainly, I would be bored to tears after the first few weeks. I need to have dreams that include impacting large numbers of people, creating change in cultures and communities, and going beyond my comfort zone. This book is all about helping people like you break free from cracked lenses and chase after your dreams. In fact, this book is part of my dream and one of the many steps required to achieve it.

What specific freedoms do you need to unlock before your dreams can become a reality? What limits do you feel you have in your dreaming process? Now unleash your "inner two-year-old" to explore why those restrictions might be ingrained or showing up. You have to be serious about connecting to the dreams you set.

To take a little bit of the pressure off, we will later identify where the battles may be in reflecting on who you are, your greatest skill sets, and what you are capable of taking on. The most important thing now is to connect with the freedom of dreaming and identify your wants and wishes.

I know it is challenging, but work to remove restrictions, release expectations, and, for a moment, allow yourself to forget the responsibilities that you are at times crushed by. Life has its way of derailing the dreams we once had and then restricting our ability to see future opportunities.

What parts of your life once made you feel alive and joyful? What motivations did you lock in, and what future were you chasing before the weight of bills and responsibilities crashed in? Many of us let dreams die that were meant to be part of our greater future. Take this time to reconnect with what your future dreams could hold.

Back to the Basics

People tend to overcomplicate their concepts, but you can break them down into the right steps. It is important to give yourself the right equation, recipe, and combination that will allow you to pursue and actually achieve your dream. You have to keep in check the limits you are pushing to create greater dreams. Putting the wrong fuel in a vehicle, adding the wrong ingredients to Grandma's cookie recipe, allowing the wrong foods during a weight-loss season, or trying to fish offshore with a freshwater setup will all lead to undesirable results. Almost all of us have incorrect "ingredients" or programming in our foundation that give us resistance. Here are a few quick self-reflective questions to work through:

- What aspects of your dreaming or goal setting surpass what your parents communicated or demonstrated?
- What did you hear, see, or experience that could limit your goals?
- What traumas, hardships, or difficulties have you faced that may affect your identity, skills, and potential?
- What are the comforts, securities, or safeties that you are prone to moving toward rather than challenging yourself to take greater action? Once identified, where did they stem from?
- Where are you finding limitations or roadblocks to your freedom to dream?
- What cycles or consistent patterns in your life could you identify that might indicate there's an issue with the programming inside of you?
- Which of the above cycles or patterns could hinder your dreams or goals?

Your future is built on the dreams you set for your life. That is why these fundamentals are so important.

I've noticed that whenever I struggle to elevate my skill set or push beyond my comfort zone to achieve a greater outcome, obstacles are almost always simple or something I believe I have already overcome. That is the thing about some of the past aspects of our lives: they do not haunt us consciously but rather subconsciously, shaping our actions. My older brother, who disliked any attention that diverted from him, serves as an example of an obstacle in my life. Regarding this, I must constantly keep my thoughts in check to ensure they do not affect my momentum. Thoughts about my brother became a problem whenever I achieved major milestones or earned high grades, especially during my birthday party or any celebratory gathering.

When attention was focused on me, he had a way of hijacking it, usually in a way that created embarrassment or mockery directed at me. The issue persisted consistently to the extent that I no longer desired to attend birthday parties, get-togethers, or celebrations where I was the center of attention. You would think that I could leave this in the past and that I eventually grew out of it, but that is not the case. I struggled for many years as an adult and fought against anything that created unnecessary focus on me or my achievements. I avoided celebrating major accomplishments in my business, birthday parties, and any recognition that could create the same dynamics between me and others that reminded me of the relationship between my brother and me.

As you can understand, it's something that, if not kept in check, could create a major issue when it comes to being an author, coach, keynote speaker, and someone passionate about impacting lives. When I take the stage, there is a natural focus on me and even the accolades and achievements from my past. This is why I have had to do a lot of work to reframe my circumstances and allow myself to push past those fears that any attention on me will lead to humiliation.

Even though I have done that work, I still have to keep this in check. *Am I making decisions in my goal setting, scheduling, and relationship-building based on this fear, or am I living in the freedom to chase my goal of impacting millions of people during my lifetime?* This is not something that will magically go away, and I will have to remain aware of my tendency to draw back into the shadows rather than push into the light. If not kept in check, this could have become the destruction of my ability to create and pursue my dreams.

In your life, you have to go back to the basics and leverage the questions above and the resources at the end of the book, as well as the other resources I provide in my first book, *Suck Less, Do Better*, to really dive into the aspects of your life where destructive tendencies could be. We'll explore more examples in the next chapter, but I wanted to be open about these parts of my life. The momentum you build during this process and the growth you can achieve by digging deep and challenging the core of your dreams can be a major catalyst in your life.

It is important to bring these vital aspects to the forefront as we work through the foundations of your dreams. As you can understand, I feel it is important to protect Grandma's cookie recipe and ensure that the wrong ingredients don't make their way into a single batch. Even more importantly, I take it seriously when it comes to guiding you in the right reflections and challenges in your life and dreams.

It Doesn't Have to Be

Just because it once was doesn't mean it has to be what continues. This thought always brings about a different aspect of freedom and challenges our dreams. Each of us lives in the habits, processes, and ingrained automaticities of our past, and I feel we tend to forget that we have absolute control over our lives and what people would consider our destiny.

Rather than thinking in terms of a destiny, I prefer to live in the concept of the culmination of my greatest goals, ambitions, outcomes, and purpose-filled actions, which I define as my "lighthouse." I will not delve deeply into the details of how to set your lighthouse and what should or could be included, but I will explore this a little further in Chapter Six. I explore different aspects of this in my book *Suck Less, Do Better*. I highly recommend connecting to this concept and creating the "lighthouse" for your life.

This future in front of you is an incredible opportunity to change the course of your direction and lay a new foundation that will be the launchpad for your new dreams. To some, it might feel almost wrong to challenge our automatic responses and default pressures, but there is no reason to continue living your life as if it is the culmination of others' lives and requirements placed on you by other people.

The idea that "what was doesn't have to continue to be" frees us from the chains of the past. We can learn from the past and change our habits, expectations, and processes. I know it's easier said than done, but remember that we're in the chapter on challenging your dreams. Consider this: if you do not question the status quo and begin to think about whether you want it to continue, it will remain unchanged by default.

This is something even a Disney princess could lock into. In the 2015 movie *Cinderella*, Cinderella states, "Just because it's what's done doesn't mean it's what should be done!" to try to stop Prince Charming from killing an animal. (Also, so no one takes this the wrong way, I am not against hunting, and this is not some subtle political jab; it's just a funny quote and a way to connect to a positive idea about change.)

Walking away from what we are accustomed to is very tough, and once you become aware of your default tendencies, it can feel like unstable ground. The more you explore this, the more you see that you are a mix of actions and behaviors, along with the limits of others' expectations and their demands for your life.

I know this firsthand and understand that it can rock you a bit, but don't stress. I will not leave you hanging. Later in the book, you will create the version of yourself that is displayed, allowing you to connect with the core of what you are meant to take on and accomplish in your life. I'm excited about what we'll explore later in this book, but if I don't help you take a step back and start questioning your dreams and how you see yourself, your future, and your opportunities, you won't be ready to go deeper.

One thing I want you to understand is that I don't have anything to gain from you stepping back, challenging everything in your life, and setting more incredible goals. I won't benefit from you challenging your automatic responses, beliefs, expectations, or the achievements you are capable of taking on.

This is one of the hardest parts of getting advice, especially from friends or family. There always seem to be ulterior motives, whether conscious or subconscious. They either want to profit from your success or have a specific idea of how you should succeed. There are some cases where, if you really succeed, they might feel less about themselves, so they give you advice that will keep you one step behind them.

I tell my consulting and coaching clients that I want them to be more successful than I am. I want to leverage my twenty years of experience to fast-track their success so they can achieve even more in their lifetime. I want to build people up and get them dialed in to take on challenges that even I have yet to take on. If the people around me are succeeding, I feel charged up and empowered to go out and change more lives.

I am here to break down the barriers to my success I have encountered: lessons I had to learn the hard way and concepts I have spent countless hours studying and learning to apply to gain traction. I have also used these same concepts in mastermind groups and one-on-one coaching sessions, and I have had great success helping clients break through to higher levels of outcomes. Why wouldn't I break this down for you and have you work through challenging the past and your dreams so you can revisit the core of who you are and what you are chasing after?

Don't Lose the Battle Before It Begins

The concept of starting with the end in mind is a principle I apply in business and many other areas of my life. Think about it as defining the investment of your time, effort, and actions. This will help you ensure your momentum stays aligned with the end result you are chasing. When you have your ending locked in and centered in your mind, it helps you create a more focused approach to maximize results from your actions.

Let's look at it from the perspective of your long-term goals, ambitions, and outcomes that you are currently challenging yourself to achieve. What if these are not properly identified or even misconstrued? Would that create any issues with your long-term output and capabilities? Would that lessen or divert your ability to take greater action?

Not challenging your dreams, goals, and ambitions can leave you chasing something well below your full potential. For some of you, it will leave you chasing others' dreams, ambitions, and expectations they have placed on you. You cannot lose the battle before you've even begun. This requires a disruption in your mental processing. Just taking the time to challenge these aspects might be enough to give you a clearer line of sight of what you want your life to be, what outcomes you need to achieve, and how you want your story to be read.

The hardships on your success journey are difficult, but even more so are the hardships on a success journey that isn't really yours. This is why I encourage you to take these moments, challenge everything, and then rebuild the structures and layouts of your dreams. Your life is your own, and the dreams you should be fighting for should only be yours. How much harder will you push, how much deeper will you sacrifice, and how much greater will you perform when you are fully aligned with the dreams you've defined by first challenging the *why* behind them?

CHAPTER 4

Where Is the Battle?

"What am I doing, Nate? I don't know what is wrong with me." Eddie's words rang through the room like a loud bell, but the realization of the constant spiral of destruction was the overwhelming focus. This moment was a confrontation with the habits, hurt, unresolved issues, and actions that were causing the failure of his business and financial life and the destruction of his dreams.

The circumstances he found himself in during this phase were a mix of normal business struggles and difficulties magnified by impulsive decisions made along the way. These decisions and the financial hardships combined created an insurmountable roadblock in his journey to stabilize and continue in business, not to mention to invest in the future growth of his company.

As we worked to identify any consistent trends or deep-rooted drivers, it became clear that he had broken internal wiring, driving his impulsive decisions and causing a lack of focus in areas that could cause failure in difficult seasons.

Diving into the situation with Eddie, we reviewed the past 120 days leading up to this meeting. He found that there was a decline in leads for his service-based company. The schedule for the next few weeks wasn't looking as full as he would like, and he felt the pressure to keep his team of around twenty people busy and profitable.

Eddie followed the normal process by calling his marketing service provider, lighting them up, and instructing them to take action and step up their fulfillment. He also made a few phone calls to his office staff to make sure that all phone systems and lead channel management were working properly. After handling these few phone calls, Eddie returned to his usual daily routine, just hoping the marketing team would deliver better results.

As the weeks progressed, the issue persisted and even worsened, and his team was running out of work to sustain the number of employees he had on staff. This led to tough decisions to let go of a few of his team members, which triggered an emotional response that made him feel he was failing as a leader, business owner, and man. You would think this would be enough to drive him to a stronger call to action, make adjustments to his marketing plan, and even consider deeper referral relationship development or other aspects of lead generation. This was not the case for Eddie; he not only stuck his head in the sand, hoping the same process that had been failing would sort itself out, but also started down a path of a series of impulsive decisions that created additional financial burdens.

Within the next 60 days, Eddie decided to purchase a new high-end sports car, upgrade his wife's vehicle to one priced more than twice their current one, and buy a Rolex watch with an over-$10,000 price tag. This all occurred during a season when he disconnected from the daily operations of his business, leaving his staff to manage the team and creating financial difficulties from the downturn in clients, which his new decisions had exacerbated.

Eddie's personal life decisions compounded the business's financial difficulties, perpetuating a cycle of insanity and creating an unmanageable level of stress. He was frantically moving money around and selling potential income-producing work vehicles, desperate for every penny. This also led to the release of even more billable team members and other costly decisions, ultimately causing major destruction within the company.

As Eddie and I sat and worked through the deep aspects of these last crazy 120 days, I was more focused on the feelings experienced and the actions that followed. The depth of this conversation was incredible, and it led to many angles on the internal issues driving his decisions. Talking about the initial point of decline triggered in him a sense of failure and the fear that he was on the path back to poverty. This was so crippling that he felt he couldn't see through it, and he didn't have the mental bandwidth to dig deep and reconnect with the business.

Eddie explained that what he had now grown accustomed to, defined as success, and took pride in was the ability to be more of a hands-free owner of a company that was growing. If he had gone back to being fully involved in the business, it would have felt like a regression in his life, a loss of what he now regarded as success. So he distanced himself further from the business to maintain his emotional state and sense of success.

When the issues grew to the point that he could no longer ignore them and had to eliminate team members, it triggered an even deeper sense of failure, as he felt he'd let these people down. This created a reaction that most of us cannot relate to: the pursuit of a greater sense of success by going out and spending money as if he had an unlimited supply.

Running from his real problems and looking for an emotional coping mechanism left him seeking a dopamine hit, which led to the new vehicle and Rolex purchases. It probably fulfilled his emotional needs for the moment, but it created other cash-flow issues, including debt and monthly bills. Walking around with the shiny new watch on his arm may have gained him some attention from his peers, but the fact that his entire financial life was on fire and he was only adding fuel to it wasn't even on his radar.

Eddie was driven to take actions that would help him maintain the feeling of success without facing the reality of his tough financial situation. The emotional patches he was using were only temporary, and greater destruction resulted. Together, we uncovered his fear of failure, his need to prove others wrong, his longing to be accepted, and many other driving forces that were fueling his decisions.

In these moments, his emotional side drove him most, and his inability to step back and gain a broader perspective on his actions and decisions prompted him to seek a solution to his feelings. The programming inside him and all the other factors at play created a disaster that was a bigger problem than just a revenue decrease in the business. The compounding effects he created by failing to lock in and put the required time, focus, and strategy into his business dominoed alongside the financial decisions, almost costing him his entire business and even the dreams he had been chasing.

Eddie's real experience is one of many examples of the internal programming issues faced by entrepreneurs, business owners, and executives I've worked with. Some of the programming inside each of us may have contributed to our current point, whether good or bad, but it holds us back from pursuing the greatest future we are capable of.

You might think you aren't that far gone and are way too intelligent or experienced to make these kinds of mistakes. This isn't where it all started for Eddie; it wasn't the first time this cycle happened to him, though this was the first time when the issue was on that large a scale.

Also, this is one of countless ways past issues can surface and create destruction in our lives. Indeed, this situation is extreme and serves as a prime illustration of how a problem can escalate to a significant extent. However, it's common for us to encounter internal forces that influence our decisions without pausing to contemplate and inquire about the reasons behind them. This moment in Eddie's life required him to face a tough reality and acknowledge that his actions were causing the destruction of his dreams and everything he had worked so hard for. If he were not ready to confront these subconscious driving forces as well as his emotions and work to reprogram the way he was processing each of them, he would have continued to spiral toward destruction in his business and financial life.

The point Eddie found himself in is something I have had to face personally many times in my own journey, even though the situation might not have been as drastic. If I hadn't addressed these subconscious driving forces and emotions, they would have severely hindered my ability to realize the dreams I had set for myself. I have had to reflect on my actions and identify the ones that are not aligned with the goals and ambitions I am pursuing, as well as the disruptive behaviors driven by fear, insecurity, or any internal broken programming.

Early in my entrepreneurial journey, I had dreams I was passionate about, but a constant anchor held me back from taking the actions required to reach them. I had to push hard to connect to each aspect of my life and dig deep into why I had such resistance to the required actions I needed to take. There were so many times when I had to step back, revisit the initial dreams I set, and challenge myself to dream beyond what I could imagine. The limitations and derailments often seemed overwhelming, but I was willing to be open about not only my attributes and skill sets but also the programming that led me to get off track and self-destruct. During that part of my journey and to this day, I have had to do the hard work of navigating these aspects and becoming more self-aware at every stage of growth, ambition, and achievement to ensure I am not holding myself back so I can push forward without resistance.

Too often, instead of paying attention to their own dreams, some people look at where others are succeeding. They compare themselves and let others' lives derail their journey. I have seen the constant cycles of frustration and disruption created by competing with those around you and by seeking their approval.

The harsh truth we all must confront is that the struggle we encounter on this journey is not external, but internal. Yes, external factors may cause friction or pressure, but it ultimately depends on how we allow them to impact us. You must own your thoughts, actions, and how outside influences shape your life.

There are aspects of your past and programming that have been instilled in you by your parents, groups, and other influences in your life. These are cracked lenses that can create major distortions in how you see yourself, drive you to take derailment-inducing actions, and limit how you pursue your future. You have to decide whether to continue allowing them to have control or to become disciplined in the process of acknowledging, reframing, and overcoming them to avoid the cycles of insanity they can create in your life.

If you dwell on your past instead of learning how to leverage experiences for your future, the next phase of your life will suffer. It will be marked by false starts, flawed plans, and a lack of real momentum. It is easy to see how things might not be fair or how it might feel like the world is out to get you as you sit and lick your wounds like a battered dog. This will not give you any growth, leverage, or development for a better future.

That's why I think it's important for you to see that the battle is always within you. Even in the most difficult times I have faced, I forced myself to identify the areas I could control and the aspects I could learn from and leverage. The first area of control was managing how I viewed the obstacles in my life and changing my perspective. I extracted every ounce of the lessons so I could help others down the road when they face hardship.

Don't get me wrong; there were moments when I felt as though I was getting picked on by life, and I hit some walls of extreme frustration, but what kept me from going down the self-pity walkway was knowing that I could leverage the experiences to make a difference. I knew that the only way to survive some of these situations and hope to thrive on the other side was to fight the battle inside my head.

This principle is foundational, not just during your struggles and hardest times but in all your circumstances and action steps. Your childhood wiring, programming, and other default mindsets must be addressed and kept in check. Navigating and conquering these drivers, motivators, derailers, and potential holdbacks is the path to victory.

Awareness Required

To live a life filled with dreams, ambitions, and the drive to chase them down will require a great deal of awareness and your ability to recognize your cracked lenses, coupled with the ability to identify areas where holdbacks have shaped your progress and actions.

Your journey is unique, but there are common themes that have held back many people I have worked with. These factors include facets of fear, such as the fear of failure, fear of not being accepted, fear of being rejected, fear of asking for help, and other fears. Another factor is what I call the "feel like" group: *I feel like I am not good enough, I feel like I am an imposter, I feel like my dreams are ridiculous or a bit crazy*, and *I feel like I won't be able to rise to the demands required of me.* Then you have guilt-based factors: *Am I being self-focused? Am I being greedy? How will my success make other people feel?* This is before you get to the more general factors, such as limiting beliefs, uncertainty about whom to trust, difficulty facing hard truths, and resistance to being open and vulnerable.

Chasing greatness and presenting yourself as your best self may seem like a challenging journey filled with emotions, problems, and emotional baggage. Have you ever taken the time to really analyze why it can feel this way? I am talking about a comprehensive review of your holdbacks, feelings, mental challenges, and everything that might be behind the way you constantly feel stuck. Some of these are conscious, but many run in our subconscious and can affect how we show up every day and in various situations.

Remember that tool about getting in touch with your "inner two-year-old." It is all about the deep-rooted "why." It may not be sexy, but it works if you use it to reach your deepest feelings, emotions, and motivations. Some of these are not beneficial, while you can channel others to be leveraged for good. To better control how you act, react, and are influenced by these drivers, it's vital to connect to each of these aspects and understand where they come from.

Your growth and development depend on your awareness and understanding of each of them, but even if these issues stem from an individual or your childhood, it doesn't change where the battle is. The battle is and will always be within you, and only with you. You may need to set boundaries with some people, but you must overcome how your past is affecting your present.

To put this in perspective and help you visualize how these might be affecting you, imagine a runner pushing through a marathon. This feat is difficult and requires training, nutrition, and planning, but think how much more difficult it would be if the runner strapped on a vest with a hundred small parachutes attached. This would create severe drag and even pull the runner in directions that are not aligned with the goal of completing the marathon.

Now, think about your past issues, mindsets, misdirected mental processes, inability to see yourself for who you are capable of becoming, etc., as those small parachutes. They are all attached to your back as you chase your dreams and strive to reach your full potential. I find that most people are largely unaware that these distractions are attached to them and affect their movement and performance. This is why working to gain awareness in your life is a major and pivotal step in your process, and it only comes through self-reflection in order to find these connections.

These issues can take different forms or behaviors in our lives but are fundamentally at the core of the issues many of us face, actively derailing our momentum. Early in my entrepreneurial journey, my life became extremely derailed by comparing myself to other entrepreneurs who launched their businesses around the same time as mine. This comparison and rating of my performance always seemed like a rigged system: I would focus on the greater attributes of someone else's business or leader, I would beat myself up over my weaknesses in those areas, get derailed, and become frustrated about what I considered failures. I also found myself in competition with people I hadn't even signed up to compete against, a battle set up for my defeat.

I put all of this into a group I call "noise": distractions that derail my focus. I took time to connect the dots in my childhood, find the point in my life when I had been programmed to take on challenges I was destined to fail at, and compare myself with others using a weighted scoring system that would ensure my loss. Once I started working through the process of identifying the fundamental areas this could stem from, it became abundantly clear that it was a pattern I was recreating from my childhood.

From a very young age, I was in a constant competition I didn't sign up for, a rigged system that guaranteed my loss against my older brother. My focus was always on areas he was strong in, which also happened to be my weaknesses. This led to my glorification of other people's strengths and my inability to celebrate my strengths. Talk about a major point of failure in my life, an ongoing process that was a quick route toward a constant wall of shame and self-defeating actions.

This situation from my early life might not have been drastic, but the programming it created developed habits and responses that derailed my progress without me even being aware of it. My early programming will differ from yours, but it shows how these situations can have an effect on your future.

This is where the awareness is of grave importance; this is where it all starts. I can tell you concepts and wow you with my ability to tell connective stories, but until you are ready to dive into the awareness aspect of your growth, there will always be actions that pull you away from your full potential. We all have cracked lenses hindering our progress, and until we choose to acknowledge them, they will be points of contention on our journeys.

Find hope in this process and begin to recognize your true self, the limitless opportunities ahead, and the strengths you already possess. The realness that comes through this process allows you to move forward free from the nagging aspects ingrained in you from the past.

Choose to Take Control

A defining moment is what's needed. I am not talking about a manufactured moment of feelings. In the most serious of ways, you need to decide to take control of your life. This means taking full ownership of your actions, behaviors, and issues that you bring to the table, and not allowing yourself to fall into the default reactions that have allowed them to rule your days.

This is a moment when you say to yourself, "Enough is enough." You decide not to let your past control how you show up or how your future is defined. This is a deliberate choice to take back control of who you are becoming and how you will show up, maximizing the potential life you can create for yourself.

The easy answer is to keep going through life with the same modus operandi, but you must look at your history and prior track record. Will you be happy if your past is the same as your future?

Even though I have done some great things in the past, I will be honest with you: I don't want these to be the greatest things I accomplish in my life. I hope to achieve more. This is my one shot at making a difference and having an impact, and if I allow all my limiting beliefs and holdbacks to keep me down like I have in the past, then I will go to my deathbed with major regrets.

This is why I have decided to take full control, keep it, and get uncomfortable. This isn't easy for me, writing this book and putting so much about my past, my issues, and my failures out there for so many people to read, pick apart, and possibly mock me for. Of course, I am tempted to keep to myself, use the money I've earned from my business, and travel for the rest of my life, creating only unforgettable memories. However, what impact can I have if I approach life with such negligence?

My future demands that I decide to be either fully in or fully out; there is no in-between. If you don't take full control, you're letting your past control you. I know it isn't easy or comfortable. Nothing that brings greatness in life is discovered, created, or achieved through ease and comfort.

You can look back and feel sorry for yourself all you want and think you are owed for all you have been through, but that will never get you to a better future. You can wait for a golden ticket to fall into your hand based on your story or luck, but I will tell you that the gateway to your best future requires you to push through the discomfort and do the hard things. The rewards of the better life you are chasing require the decision to take control of the cracks in your lenses and never look back.

Who You Are vs. Who You Intended to Be

There is a major difference between how you are showing up in your life right now and who you are intended to be. Each of us has baggage from our past that creates masks we wear, behavioral changes, and even the complete dismantling of our personalities in some cases. The raw truth is that life often complicates how we show up, and most of the time, it starts at an early age. The environments we are raised in, the cultures we are born into, the expectations instilled in us, the brokenness of our parents, and so many other aspects mold and shape who we become.

Take a step back and consider these reflections: Have you allowed your cracked lenses and your hurt, trauma, and hardships to change and define you? Have you adapted from the person you were intended to become because of outside factors?

Let's get a little deeper here. I am not taking away from the fact that God can use tough situations, including even trauma, for good, so please don't assume anything about my consideration of how God can leverage such things. I am talking about the perspective of the natural gifts, abilities, personality traits, and other strengths you have that make you who you are. What has happened in your life that has changed the way you show up? It might be out of alignment with how you were naturally meant to be maximized.

These adaptations can take the form of playing a sport you never felt you were equipped to play, but a parent made a point of making sure you participated. What about the school you attended, or didn't attend? The people you dated or married, the way you handled your health, weight, or nutrition, and what about the way you handle your finances, career choices, and future planning? I have seen this in almost every form.

One person in my mastermind group, a man almost 50 years old, broke down during our process and realized he had been living his entire life according to expectations his family had placed on him. In the end, he discovered he was living his life as his father, mirroring his father's personality and strengths rather than living in the greatness he could achieve with his own skill sets and abilities. He and his father were very different, but because of the expectations and demands put on him, he changed the entire way he showed up and became almost exactly like his father to gain approval and acceptance.

This situation is more common than you think, especially when it comes to minor changes made to gain the approval of parents or others. We are influenced by those around us, and most of us want to fit in. This means some aspects of the adaptation we take on reduce the natural self, so we take on differing actions deemed more acceptable. These changes start at a young age and continue through our adolescent and school years until we reach the end, when we are filled with so many expectations and demands that it is hard to know who the "real us" is versus the version we have adapted.

When we are young, our parents use the excuse of guiding and directing us, and in many cases, that is important when it comes to right, wrong, safety, and other key factors. The issue is that parents may overstep and put expectations, direction, and their wants and wishes on us. I am not saying this is done maliciously, at least for the most part, but there can be a lack of awareness among many parents about how their words affect their children.

As an adult, you must shed the expectations, norms, and examples you grew up with. You must confront every part of your life and connect with your core, your purpose, and your beliefs. This allows you to create your hopes and dreams to achieve even greater heights than you have been programmed to.

There is freedom in this aspect when we realize who we are naturally born to become. We are built to chase our own goals and dreams. Leveraging the gifts within us can lead to major life breakthroughs and success. Yes, this requires questioning and challenging aspects that many people are not ready for, but through the process, you will become even more sure of what you believe, what you are capable of, and what you should take on in your lifetime. The life you have been called to is different from the life you have found yourself in; it is not flooded with the programming and expectations of other people. Instead, your best future should be based on your best self.

New Awareness Requires New Action

This chapter covers a lot of ground, giving you many examples and stories of how cracked lenses and other factors can disrupt how you show up and who you become. I need to give you a checkpoint and a reflective point. This information isn't something that you just read through and park on a shelf for a later day. These areas in your life require direct, urgent, and focused attention. To avoid reverting to your old programming, you'll need to create new checks and balances.

I have been purposeful in inviting people into my life who keep me in check. They ask me hard questions about the actions I am taking to keep driving toward my greatest potential. They hold me to the fire about getting uncomfortable, about not cowering, and about not letting the safety of the shadows draw me in. When you grasp the topics discussed here and think about how others, your past, or your traumas have affected you, something must change.

Some of you reading this are thinking you have everything under control and that your future is locked in. You have planned everything out and have contingencies waiting just in case. If so, I hope that your goals and ambitions have been challenged to determine whether that is the greatest potential your life has.

I know I still have not seen the full potential of what God has in store for my life. Yes, I have walked a road with a lot of trauma, hardships, failures, and what others would deem incredible wins. However, this isn't the end, and I am built to take on so much more with the days left to me. I push every day to gain new awareness and take new actions that will drive me toward a better future than I could have ever imagined.

Some of you reading this right now might pride yourselves on the number of books you read annually or consider it a badge of honor to chew through the many books each month, quarter, or year. The one thing that anyone progressing down the path to success should realize is that it doesn't matter what you read; what matters is how you take the time to apply what you learn.

Let me be snarky for a minute. I once saw a post by someone I know who presents himself with great confidence, brags about all his wins, and always seems to have something judgmental to say about other entrepreneurs. He showed a picture of about ten business-related books, all with heavy action steps, and claimed to have read them all within the first quarter of the year. He was asking for suggestions for more books, and I couldn't help myself. I posted, *"My advice is to go back and actually work through each of those books and apply the concepts step by step. This will take you more than the remainder of the year."*

I understand that each book isn't 100 percent for everyone. There might be only 20 percent or more of each book that applies to our lives, but the application process is what is missed the majority of the time. When I was starting my first business, I didn't have access to any coach or consultant; I was running like a wild stallion and doing my best at each turn. What I did was immerse myself in reading many books to gain wisdom from individuals who had advanced beyond my current level of business and leadership. I would apply the book's principles to my life and business before moving on to another book.

Some of us experience moments of overwhelm when faced with a book or guide that moves quickly and covers a vast amount of information. This should not be the point at which we keep reading but instead work to apply the most fundamental aspect. If you don't know where to start, the inner two-year-old is always a useful launch tool.

Start asking yourself about the "why" behind every behavior and action, and ask yourself why you are drawn to specific careers, jobs, businesses, financial gains, and even the people around you. Keep tracing all your behaviors and actions back to the root source. Make a list of these and work more deeply to understand how they are currently affecting you and the actions you are taking. This is especially true when it comes to how you view yourself, your potential, and how you can maximize your future. You can't skip this chapter or the important topics it covers and expect to unlock your future's full potential.

It is very important that, as you move through this book, you are a person of action and dedicated to growth. We are going to move into a section of the book that lays out action steps, tools, and self-reflective assignments. As I have expressed, I am a person of major action, and I am dedicated to impacting lives. As part of my mission, I strive to add significant value to everything I do, concentrating on areas where people can gain momentum or overcome holdbacks in their lives.

I am going to push you to get uncomfortable and look at yourself and life from new perspectives. We are going to walk through this together, and I want you to know that the reason I am so passionate about all of this is that my life had so many holdbacks before I became aware of them. I didn't have anyone to lay the foundation for me or guide me to these neuropsychological concepts or connect the dots back to my childhood and experiences. I just started trying to figure out what was wrong with me.

The path of discovery led to more than I could have imagined, and I lay it all out for you to help you fast-track your progress and save you years of struggle. The battleground is still inside of you. Will you act on this new information, or will your future be the same?

Hold the Line

All too often, we lose the battle in our thoughts, mindsets, beliefs, and actions. Establishing a connection between these issues and their origins, as well as the actions of others who may have contributed to their existence, should never be used as an excuse to surrender to defeat. The past can never be changed, and what has occurred will never be undone, but now the choice is yours: how will you identify, navigate, and learn to make the most of every next step?

Understanding how the past creates cracked lenses, convoluted mindsets, and many derailed actions is a major part of your growth and can serve as a catalyst for change. You do have to be determined to hold the line on this battleground. You must draw the line in the sand and commit to working through your past. You must identify the areas of holdbacks, limitations, and convolutions in the way you see yourself, your future, and the dreams you expect to live out.

I understand that, many times in this process, you will be kicking up feelings and emotions, and you will have to address and even wrestle with them. The process is not easy, and I would be lying if I told you that working through the pain and the hurt doesn't leave you revisiting the darkness in some moments, but the outcome of being able to release some of these things is freeing.

William Wallace is known for many dynamic sayings, but the one that hits me the hardest is *"Every man dies. Not every man really lives,"* meaning that life without freedom is not really living.

How many of us are actually living in the full freedom that is available to us? We experience no significant governmental or other major oppression, and we do not live daily in a war-ridden physical environment, but we allow this lack of freedom because our past restricts our ability to fully live.

Freedom is found only by removing limitations and living how we were originally built, called, or born to live. Continuing to allow these hardships, programming, and cracked lenses to dictate the outcome of our lives is unacceptable.

You have to make the decision to remain dedicated to fighting the battle where it really exists: deep inside you.

CHAPTER 5

Use the Frame

Sitting in the corner of my living room for hours, I stared at the wall and asked God what I had done to piss Him off. I could not wrap my mind around what had happened in my life over the prior six months. I frequently found myself on the floor in a corner, trying to make sense of everything that had occurred, questioning everything in my life, and grasping to understand even one part of it all.

I had just recovered from paralysis months prior and felt like my moment for a comeback was teed up, but instead, I was facing major heart issues and what doctors told me was a degenerative issue that would shorten my life expectancy to around ten years. Talk about a royal kick to the teeth when I felt as though I was finally building momentum again in my life.

At that moment, I was struggling with every aspect of my life, trying to fully comprehend my medical challenges and feeling tired of seeing the look of pity on people's faces when they learned about the issues I was facing. My career had just been obliterated, my health destroyed, and I was struggling with my relationship with God. He became the easy one to blame for it all in my moments of weakness and lack of understanding.

Through this season, I felt as though the darkness of life had rolled in, and I was being crushed under the pressure. I had withdrawn from almost everyone I knew because I hated the constant questions I didn't have answers to and didn't want to revisit all that had happened. The people I spent the most time with were the medical staff at the various facilities that used me as a research subject to understand what had happened to me.

To keep from falling into a depression, I pushed myself by creating new plans for my life and working to cast a new vision incorporating these changes and the potential ten-year clock. The gut-wrenching days that passed started to grind on my spirit and beat me down in ways I could have never imagined. The weight on me felt like it could not be lifted, no matter what I did or how hard I tried to distract myself.

I will be completely honest with you, as I promise to always be open and vulnerable. These moments included times when I had to fight not to let the darkness take over and make the choice to end it all. There were many times when I didn't know if I wanted to keep fighting. I hit the hardest wall and wasn't sure I wanted to get back up.

These were some of the most challenging times I have gone through, and at twenty-two years old, I was unequipped to walk through these dark roads. I say this to remind you that you're not alone in these moments and that you must keep going; an incredible life awaits you on the other side of the darkness.

In the midst of all of this, I felt that God made it clear to me that what I was fighting through and the road I was traveling wasn't just for me. I had to walk this road, learn the lessons, and fight this battle to impact people who are going through and recovering from their darkest days. The perspective within me started to shift. I hoped for more than just surviving my health situation or overcoming my financial struggles; I wanted more than just making it through.

This was a change of my entire vantage point; I would even say this was a moment of grace from God. He allowed me to see a vision of what I could do on the other side of all the mess I was in. Please don't take this to mean I had this incredible faith during that time; that was not the case. I was rather frustrated and upset with God, and we had many direct conversations that I am not proud of. I questioned Him and aspects of my faith, and I pouted like a little kid until I was able to fully grasp how the situations could be used in my life and for others.

The moments of living in these types of hard times are some of the most challenging when you feel that all the dreams and ambitions that you have set for your life are now scrambled eggs, and you are not sure what to do with them all. I won't take away your feeling of impossible positive outcomes or the flood of thoughts that encumber your every moment, but I will help you find a new perspective that could change your mindset.

This is one of the ways I like to discuss using a different frame for how you view the situation or circumstances. It is all too easy to look at the situations that we find ourselves in from a victim perspective, an "it's not fair" perspective, or other derogatory angles. During life's challenges, I often find that I feel sorry for myself, but I understand that this perspective is not beneficial for either myself or anyone else involved.

This is why I have challenged myself since my early twenties to reconsider the frame through which I view situations, difficulties, traumas, and even people. I am not saying it is always easy, but it requires me to step back and choose how I will view each of them with a different perspective.

Connect to the Frame

The concept of the frame can vary widely among people, as we all have different backgrounds. With my law enforcement background, I view my perspective as a building with many windows, and I might have to check the angles from each until I find the one with the best vantage point. If you are into art, then maybe it is the right frame with the right glass that draws attention to the exact attributes of the piece. If you are a super-nerd, used as an endearing term, and connect to the use of scientific tools like magnifying glasses and microscopes, then think about it from that aspect.

You have the power to choose your perspective, even in the most difficult moments. Think of a "frame" as a mental checkpoint, a way to pause and evaluate the vantage point from which you view your life. We all have a default way of processing hardship that shapes our emotions, but our first instinct isn't always the most accurate or correct way to view the circumstance.

While your past has inevitably shaped the lens through which you see your potential, changing your viewpoint allows you to repair the cracks. This frame concept is a tool for reflection, allowing you to swap angles and magnifiers until you find clarity. The pause and refresh are incredibly important when you are living in a situation and walking through the darkness, but it is also important to look back at past situations that are still affecting how you show up and see yourself.

I am sure you have heard people say that in every argument there are three sides: the two people involved and the truth. This is because each of us brings all of our preconceived ideas about these circumstances and disagreements. Also, we know our intentions, but the other person is not aware of what is in our hearts. This might be a bit of an exaggeration, but I will give us all the benefit of the doubt in the concept development.

We also don't know all the intentions and preconceptions that the other party brings to the argument or issue. This is what convolutes communication and, many times, creates disruption. This isn't a marriage book, and I'm not perfect at communicating in my marriage, but think of all the past arguments and identify the assumptions made or reactions heightened by preconceptions. These are all frames, perspectives, and programming within us, shaped by our past experiences, background, and prior relationships.

This is why I am pushing hard to ensure that you understand the concept of a frame. Major growth begins when you learn to step back and intentionally choose the vantage point from which you view the circumstances and hardships of your life. This helps you control how they shape your identity and future.

It's not about changing the past or controlling how others take ownership of the situation. It's about you taking control of how you will process and move forward on the other side of the difficulties you have faced.

Leverage Matured Vantage Point

I understand the title of this section might be making some assumptions, but I have faith in you that you are a work in progress and are developing and growing, which includes your maturity. The reason why this is important to consider is that when we go through circumstances, hardships, and especially traumas, we have a way of processing them, allowing them not only to affect us during those times but also to make adjustments to our programming. This is not always a bad thing, as overcoming hardships can give us more courage and confidence to take on more challenges in life.

The truth, though, is that the way we process and are affected by negative situations can create programming that might have us draw back or be more security-focused. Every experience we have shapes and programs us. Going back to childhood, think about all the programming that was instilled in you. Now take a few moments to reflect on how much of that programming was based on what is best for you as a person, specifically on how you are wired, including your skill sets and abilities.

Consider the example of parents who set expectations for their child to become a wrench-turner. They might say something like, "Son, our family is great with our hands, but the whole school thing and college thing have never been what we are best at." Then you have the parents who are more focused on their children excelling as athletes or in their academics than what they were built to take on. Others make it clear which schools are acceptable to attend and which careers are deemed less respectable. All of this does not take into consideration what potential opportunities could be the best fit for the child. It isn't about the child but about the parents and their background or programming.

The simple way my father pushed me to find a job or career with a retirement or pension program could have been a major deterrent to sticking to my dreams of taking the entrepreneurial road. Even though his communication was out of love and protecting me financially, this could have become the cracked lens that broke my dream. This was all based on his past, his experiences, and the safety that he felt he needed. I would argue that he was probably fighting with some cracked lenses from his past, which led to the heightened priority of this security.

I could give countless examples of areas, sayings, and even great-hearted people who have derailed the dreams of others through well-intentioned efforts. This is why you have to reflect and use your now more mature lens to view and challenge all the expectations, fears, motivations, and even the "why" behind everything you are pushing for, to make sure that you are not being driven by someone else's good-intentioned "crack producers."

Let's push even further into this concept and talk about trauma and consider the way we need to navigate past situations that we encountered.

The way that your brain handles and processes past trauma and similar experiences is completely different than how it processes normal memories. An automatic response occurs through the brain and nervous system in that they remain on high alert for danger, whether physical or emotional. There are so many ways this can create negative effects in our lives.

I am not saying that processing traumatic experiences through a new vantage point with more maturity will always create a release of your automatic responses, but understanding that we all have these automatic responses is a must in your awareness. I highly recommend pushing into these automatic responses and reflecting on how they could be affecting you across every area of your life.

Working to take new action and being very purposeful about how you allow your thoughts to navigate the past are important, and identifying emotional triggers and learning to control your reactions can become catalysts for your growth. Awareness and purposeful reflection can help you gain great traction in identifying where these exist in your life. After all the disasters I've been through, I know I must be aware of my surroundings and my reactions to environmental stressors. But with a lot of reframing work, I've had much success in ensuring these do not become holdbacks in my life.

Awareness alone is not enough; understanding the vantage points and frames of reference for our past experiences is what creates change. We must realize how our behaviors relate to our experiences. This requires digging to the root of where these patterns originate, staying aware of the triggers and reactions they produce, and deliberately choosing actions that help reprogram how we process them.

This is all a lot, and to be clear, I am advising against working through these issues alone without mental health professionals. I am an advocate of getting the right team around you to provide the greatest support. You must enter any of these professional engagements knowing that these people are guides on your journey and that it is completely up to you to do the hard work to free yourself from holdbacks. No one is a miracle worker who can do the work for you.

The clients I work with have to take consistent action as part of the engagement process, and I relentlessly push them to confront any deep-rooted setbacks they have. I ask them to identify their frame and see situations from different angles, freeing them from the harmful narrative that has shaped their actions, beliefs, and outlook.

The most important takeaway from this section is that we have the freedom and ability to work on our programming. This can be maximized by leveraging our more mature perspectives and increased ability to adjust our vantage points. Concentrate on the areas that create resistance or derail our capacity for growth and development. Just because we have reacted, handled things, or even made bad decisions in certain areas doesn't mean they need to continue.

That is the great part about growth and development: we are built to constantly adapt. We are not built to stay stagnant and remain unchanged. At this point in your life, you cannot allow the things that occurred in childhood, past relationships, and even prior environments to be the driving force for your future. It is not easy to take control; it is definitely not easy to work through the past. The more aggressively you pursue changing the way that your past affects you, the faster your future will be able to build momentum toward the greatest outcome you could ever imagine.

Are you going to allow past traumas and difficulties you have faced to create a capsule that limits and handicaps your future? Are you going to let past experiences dictate the greatest ability that you can achieve? You can't let trauma, drama, or any other hardship write your story. This is your life, your future, and you should be the only one taking control of how the pages read.

Difficult Perspectives, Potential Freedom

I hope that, at this point, you can connect with my desire to guide you in making a real change in your life. My desire is for you to be able to chase your dreams without the massive obstacles I see in countless individuals I have spoken to, consulted, or coached. Please know I don't write to gain a line of cheerleaders that create a cloud of encouragement for myself, but rather to help create a catalyst for you.

That said, this section will not earn me any brownie points with you if you go into it with the wrong mentality. The entire purpose of this section is to identify ways to free yourself from the chains of the past. These are some of the ways I have coped with what has occurred in my life, without what people might consider closure or resolution.

The ugly truth we must acknowledge is that anytime people are involved, things can get messy. I'm not saying you should forgive those who wronged you, but you must let go of what's holding you back.

I know you are already thinking, *Nate, you don't understand how bad they were or how traumatic it was.* I will tell you right now that I don't. I don't want to take anything from you, no matter how bad it was or how it affected you. I want you to use every tool available to gain a perspective that can help you grow and stop letting your past define your future. I want you to be free of the power and control that someone from your past had over your life. What matters more to you: holding onto your past and trauma, or cutting the chains that hold you back?

One perspective I find challenging to adopt is a lens of empathy or understanding for others' past circumstances. For the individuals who have created some of the deepest hurt in my life, it is easy for me to cast major judgment and think, *How could anyone ever do that to someone they claim to love?*

When I step back and consider the situation with a more open mind, without excusing what has happened or minimizing my hurt, I can look at it from a different angle and adjust the narrative I create in my head. Remember, this is never a justification for their actions. Instead, it's a way to see the situation with more reality and clarity rather than defaulting to inner reactions and the language of our inner voice. This allows us to control the automatic ways we process, or even internalize, some of what has happened.

An example is one I've previously discussed, in which my father told me he felt it best that I find a career or a job with a pension or retirement program when I told him I wanted to start a business. I could have thought, *My dad doesn't believe in me and thinks I am a failure who can't succeed in business.* I could also have taken it as a sign that *he doesn't think I will be good with money and will make bad financial decisions that will leave me unable to retire.* I could also have assumed that my dad felt I was too weak of a leader to build a team required for a successful business.

See how our minds can change the narrative? We often default to areas where we already have insecurities or issues. When I stepped back and reflected on this conversation, I came to understand that his advice stemmed from his past and the security he was working to build in his life. His focus was to guide and protect me in having a secure future, but since he had never built, grown, or scaled any businesses, this was completely outside his skill set, knowledge, and perhaps even his comfort zone at the time.

There are probably more details behind this. If I dug into it with him, I might discover stories of hardship he witnessed among his friends or other families that had struggled because of poor business decisions. It is absolutely necessary to examine different situations from multiple perspectives and work to gain empathy or even a better understanding.

This could also be true as you look back at some of your childhood experiences and issues, including how you were raised. I remember being a bit judgmental about some things my parents did or didn't allow when I was younger, but my perspective changed once I became a parent myself. This is not to say I did things the same way as my parents, but taking the time to reflect on it allowed me to better understand the situation. Also, being a parent myself has shown me that you must make decisions on the fly, using your best judgment in the moment, with no time to read a book or seek counsel. I don't want to excuse any actions that went too far with punishment or any type of abuse that you may have experienced. I mean that parents sometimes do things that have lasting effects on us, but they were doing their best with the knowledge they had.

This is where it's important to take that step back with your more mature perspective, think about how your parents were raised or what they experienced, and work to be more understanding about how some things were handled. We all have scar tissue from childhood, and people who say they don't have any probably have more things that are affecting them daily than they realize. This is why it is so vital to understand that when situations in our lives have a long-term effect on us, we can find freedom by looking at them from different angles and perspectives to gain a better vantage point.

This type of processing goes way beyond your parents and family relationships from childhood. Reflecting on how you processed and internalized past situations and how they affect you now can be a huge asset to your future success.

A major situation I came across with one of my clients was an affair that occurred in a long-term marriage that cut him deeply and had lasting effects on how he viewed himself, creating a lot of self-doubt and feelings of worthlessness. To provide some context, this was a diligent worker committed to his family's well-being who made an effort to remain present and family-focused while building his business. He was a good guy, not perfect, but with noble intentions, as he was dedicated to his family and the life he was striving to create for them.

During this season of their family's life, the wife lost her aunt, grandfather, and father in less than ninety days. This required the wife to travel frequently so she could be there to support the extended family and help them navigate the steps after their passing. The husband took care of the kids, handled most of the household responsibilities, and supported his wife's needs and flexibility during this season. Unfortunately, while the wife was back in her hometown, she reconnected with someone she had been emotionally involved with in her late teens, and that was the start of a slippery slope.

As you can understand, this situation reached a breaking point after a few months. I know I am leaving you on a cliffhanger regarding how he found out and all the drama that transpired. However, what's important to address here is that this entire situation created major issues in their relationship, especially with how the husband viewed himself. For years, he struggled with the feeling that he was just not good enough, leaving him doubting his actions. This crushed his self-esteem and changed the way he showed up in many areas of his life. The husband allowed this affair to affect him, leading to destructive internal mental processes and self-doubt.

He had to confront the lingering effects of this affair within himself, even though the relationship ended years later for other reasons. When we sat down, we first had to acknowledge all the ways he was processing his feelings and how he had worked through his shortcomings. He assumed he had caused the affair because he wasn't good enough, which had driven his wife to find another man. This situation was different, and even though self-reflection on our behavior is always beneficial, we must avoid getting stuck in the self-blame cycle, as it leads to a range of long-term effects.

We then worked through the wife's upbringing and discussed the fact that her mother had cheated on her spouse during one of her marriages, as well as other factors that could have played a role in her lack of loyalty. Then we dove into the circumstances and hardships his wife had faced leading up to the affair, such as the loss of three close family members in less than ninety days. I expressed that we were not looking to excuse anything but instead release some of the core fundamentals holding him back that had been haunting him.

It is easy to understand that during times of extreme loss, people have a tendency to shut down emotionally and not connect as well to their other loved ones. This type of situation allows areas of weakness to surface, and many people seek distractions to take their minds off the pain. This is where some people are prone to drinking. Some turn to drugs, and some chase other types of highs. For this woman, the excitement of attention, flirtation, and the novelty of a romantic escape made it hard to resist.

This doesn't excuse her behavior or take away the hurt the husband felt, but consider the two different narratives that could be at play and their potential long-term effects. If he continues to live in the "what if" mentality and beat himself up for what he thinks he could have done better, it will create a very difficult dynamic in future relationships. If he accepts blame where it is due and understands that it was outside his control and unintended, it can allow him to heal and have the fewest long-term effects possible. It will never erase the hurt, but using the right frame can help resolve it and limit the long-term damage it causes.

The takeaway from this is not in the exactness of the situation but in the ability to adjust your perspective and process if you come up against difficult times in your life. I know that many people use the saying, "Hurt people hurt people," but this is traditionally focused on people who have been hurt and have not been able to properly work and heal from it.

I find that the healing isn't always in just talking through it with someone but instead in challenging my perspective on it. I dive deep into how the circumstances are currently affecting me, then strive to shift my perspective and break free from the chains that hold me back or shape my narrative.

Look at those people in your life who have hurt you. Maybe there was someone in their past who wasn't strong enough to confront their pain, and they chose to continue the cycle of pain and destruction. This doesn't mean what happened to you is justified. However, you can look at the person who has hurt you from a different perspective, as they might have had serious issues in the past.

This doesn't change what has occurred, but it can help reduce destructive feelings and negative self-reflection so you can place responsibility where it is due and take ownership in areas you can control.

For many of us, cracked lenses arise not just from the situation but also from how we process and internalize it. Each of us has a default way of processing past situations and circumstances, which, for some, shapes the narrative of our value. This often takes ownership away from those who caused the circumstances and puts unnecessary responsibility on our shoulders. There are many situations in which we are to blame; self-inflicted wounds are great learning experiences that should not be glossed over.

What I am talking about is being intentional about the frame you use to reflect on and process the past situations and difficulties you have encountered. You always have to challenge your default perspectives and consider other vantage points that may be more applicable given the circumstances. This isn't a guaranteed fix, but changing perspectives has allowed many people to adopt a vantage point that has stopped them from continuing the cycle of self-defamation or from confirming their negative self-perceptions. This, in turn, can enable new action and an entirely new trajectory.

Many people default to perspectives that have long-term effects, leading to a slippery slope of feeling inadequate, doubting their identity, and sometimes even attempting to change to feel good enough. I can't go over every situation I've faced, but it's important to consider and question every perspective.

Each of us has our own standard vantage point for how we process the situations we encounter, but this cannot continue without us challenging and working to control our perspectives. This is why I always feel it is important to check the frame I am looking through in every situation and to control how I allow past circumstances to affect my future actions.

Those who take these moments to work through the past and even the current situations they encounter can find growth, release, and even new self-reflection by challenging the perspectives they default to. Healing can take place without having an apology or admittance of guilt from the other people involved. You have the strength, ability, and tools to work through these situations that have, in some cases, haunted you and derailed your potential.

Light in the Darkness

The great thing about frames and perspectives is that we can choose to change how we process situations and even experience tremendous growth during and after. There is a concept called "posttraumatic growth," or PTG, which has been defined by the Boulder Crest Foundation as *"A process that helps us grow in the midst of stress, struggle, hardship and trauma and a series of domains where we grow."* The Boulder Crest Foundation is an incredible not-for-profit best known for its support of veterans and first responders dealing with Post-Traumatic Stress Disorder, or PTSD.

The fifth phase of PTG centers on service. Boulder Crest Foundation goes on to explain this: *"By making sense of our experiences, we can develop the willingness and courage to share our lessons with others, enriching their lives and helping them to struggle well. We also realize, because others have been there for us, how critical it is to give back and make a positive impact in the lives of others. In the process, they grow, and so do we."*

We all have feelings we might have to confront, such as, *Why did this happen to me? What did I do to deserve this?* and, *Why couldn't this have happened to someone who is a bad person?* The reality, however, is that you and I cannot change the past, so we have to take a step back and focus on how we will leverage it.

I have been encouraged, even in my darkest days, that nothing that has happened or will happen to me is in vain. God will give me the opportunity to impact others because of what I have walked through. I have opened up to you about some of my hardest moments back in my early twenties, but the reality is that the road I have walked has been flooded with other major, crazy obstacles.

The difference is that I have been able to go through hardships with a different perspective since then. I strive to maintain a hopeful perspective in everything I face, understanding that not everything will unfold as I envision in the best-case scenario, but that I can learn, grow, and leverage my experiences within the hardship to positively impact lives on the other side.

Of course, like you, I would rather avoid walking through hard moments, but that isn't reality. I choose a mindset of taking on every challenge with the purpose of learning and growing so I can relate to and guide others through their hardships.

I found myself laughing a few months ago when a surgery I underwent led to what felt like endless complications. I wasn't sure when I would be able to use the experience to help others, but I asked God to give me opportunities. Since then, I have found that I am much more caring towards others going through surgery, as I understand how quickly they can get squirrelly. This allows me to be more purposeful about checking in on those close to me as they undergo any surgeries, even ones that are supposed to be simple.

This, coupled with quite a few other issues and hardships I faced that same year, made it rather humorous to me that I was writing a book about hardships, difficulties, and the past and how they can create cracks in our lenses and affect how we pursue our futures. God was providing opportunities for me to gather more stories to share and examples to offer.

This is what I tell myself during the most difficult times to keep my mindset in line with who I am called to be:

With God's help, I am strong enough to turn something awful into something powerful. I will not let anything that happens to me be in vain; it is up to me to maximize the impact that I can pull from the experience. Yes, I need strength from God in many situations, but I can choose to walk out my life with the intention of impacting lives with my experiences. I focus my mindset on the idea that, if it were going to be someone, it is good it was me. I can leverage any hardship or difficulty to create change, impact, or growth. I have been given the opportunity to walk through this challenge and prove that people are capable of greatness, no matter what they face.

As you know, it isn't easy to keep this my focus, and it requires great intention to stay centered in this mindset. This will almost never be a default way of looking at life's difficulties, which is why we have to be set on changing our mindsets and how we process circumstances, from the small situations to the large disasters we may find ourselves in.

The way we handle adversity is really up to us, and if you consider the light in the darkness you can bring to others, it might change how you go through hardships. Also, take time to adjust your view of the past and find ways to use it to grow, develop, and connect with those around you.

This perspective, like the others I listed above, might not be for everyone, but that is why I took the time to break them down so you can see which best applies to your life. The key here is to look at your life and the hardships you have encountered from different angles and with different lenses to gain the most clarity, freedom, and growth possible.

Control Your Controllables

At this point, we cannot go back and change what has happened to us. No matter how much we wish and want every day, the past is what it is. In your current situation, you can only focus on what you can control. The way you view the past, the way you allow it to control you, and the way you leverage it are all areas within your control.

This might be a harsh reality for some of you. It might not be what you want to hear if you are clinging to the story that you are a victim or, for some reason, find comfort in being the one who has been wronged. But if you stay in that mindset, you will lose the ability to write an incredible story with the days you have left.

The badges of honor that you have earned in those tough situations are no good if you allow them to define your life. Instead, use your past to find your life's purpose and potential. This is why, earlier in this book, I pushed you to lock in on challenging everything, and right now, doing so with your past is vital.

One of the difficulties some of us deal with is that the past isn't something we can control. We cannot go back and change the way we handle ourselves in specific situations. What we are left with are the actions we can control today: how we leverage and grow from our past experiences to create the greatest future.

This is the mentality of controlling what is within your grasp and then releasing what is outside your control. How are you processing your past and finding the growth that comes from what you've been through? What are the areas from your past that give you a specific set of skills and abilities that you can leverage to impact or serve others? Now, could some of this just be having better coping strategies? Yes, but the goal is to make sure that your past doesn't hold you back.

I know that it is within my control to find the positives in some of the most unfortunate situations I have dealt with. I feel a strong conviction to never waste any experience, and I ask God to bring people into my life whom I can impact because of what I have been through. To be clear, I am not saying you can fix all of your issues by changing your perspectives on your own, and I do strongly advise you to seek therapy, counseling, or the right team to work properly through as much of your past as possible.

Many of the people I work with have gone through therapy and still find themselves having major holdbacks, but through our process, they connect with the ability to shift their perspectives, which allows them to gain back control of their current actions and future. Others I have been able to impact are people who would never be open to traditional therapy or counseling. These perspective shifts are tools in your toolbox, and you will have to do the work, testing them out and determining which, alone or in combination, might work best for you.

The frame you choose to view the present, past, and future is crucial. If you are not purposeful in choosing your frame, you will default to perspectives based on how you were programmed from birth. Your decision to maximize your future and leverage your past experiences requires a change in the frame in which you view the life you have and will live.

This is not an easy task, and for many of us, it requires living in a constant inner battle to keep our frame in check and prevent a destructive narrative from taking over. Your future requires you to control your present perspectives, driving your mindsets and actions.

CHAPTER 6

Create Your Display

In a whirlwind of frustration, Susan yelled, "Nate, I just don't know who I am supposed to be in all of these different situations!" She'd reached the boiling point of her turmoil and ultimate exhaustion, constantly feeling like she had to morph into each relationship, event, and circumstance in her life. All of it felt like an endless game of tug-of-war against an unlimited number of opponents. She couldn't see any end in sight and was exhausted by the continued fight for acceptance.

As we pushed deeper into what was going on and how she'd gotten to this place, Susan broke down, going into the details from her childhood and how, from a very young age, she never felt good enough. Through this process, we discussed the abuse, neglect, and overly harsh ways she had been treated since as far back as she could remember.

In her childhood, Susan had constantly adapted to her parents' moods and navigated how they reacted to her actions in different circumstances. It was like riding a bike on a trail clearly marked for your travel but laid with landmines that could not be avoided. Her need for acceptance from her parents had become her driving force to figure out how they wanted her to show up and act, with no direction given and only rigid correction when she did not align with their unspoken expectations.

This was the unfortunate inspiration of Susan's need to constantly change and almost the derailment of who she was intended to be. Susan was in what felt like a constant state of change, always waiting for feedback from her parents and then others in her adult life to determine what was acceptable and what was not. The entire baseline of Susan's life was built on what others wanted or expected of her, rather than a solid foundation of who she was.

When Susan and I worked together, she was in her early fifties and about to have a major meltdown. She was pressed, feeling that she wasn't good enough for any environment she found herself in. Taking the time to track her issue all the way back to her childhood and how it showed up in every stage of her life was a painful process for her to walk through. The next steps in her life would be the ones that mattered the most.

Working backward to identify core issues and their origins is the catalyst point. The healing process requires many changes in perspectives as well as a lot of inner work. Susan had to relearn who she was and truly embrace the freedom to be herself. This critical process involved not only identifying the core of who she was but also accepting and understanding how to leverage the greatness that is her true self.

This situation was heartbreaking, and I found myself fully engulfed in supporting her through this complete overhaul and her resurfacing into the greatness of her potential. I hold Susan in high regard, and she blossomed into an extraordinary individual.

In my life and work with clients, I've learned that we all have complex self-perceptions. Susan's story is an extreme example of how childhood can have a major impact on our adult lives. This is why, earlier in this book, I provided details on the concept I call "cracked lenses" and the neuroscientific concepts behind it.

I think it's important for us all to reflect on our past and how it affects our current behavior. All these circumstances in our lives and our pasts affect how we see ourselves and the potential we have for our future. Our situations may not be as extreme as Susan's, but even the best of childhoods can still have aspects that create cracked lenses.

Instead of just focusing on helping you live a life of success, I am dedicated to assisting you in fully connecting to who you really are and unlocking your ability to achieve the greatest potential you are capable of. This requires you to examine your life from a different perspective and be willing to confront the expectations and programming instilled in you.

I am not saying that this is easy; it's hard to navigate and separate the truths from the falsities, as much of the programming was normalized and deeply rooted. This is about stripping away past hurts to reach the core of who you truly are. By building on a foundation of truth rather than old emotions, you unlock the power to create the future you were always meant for.

Raw Discovery

In my early twenties, I created a process to unlock my true potential. I was in a season of working to understand why I had made the decisions I had and what options were available to me. I was unsettled because I knew I was playing small. The path I had chosen didn't account for what I could actually achieve if I fully unlocked and applied my greatest strengths. This process of self-discovery helped me identify and clearly break down the walls that had been holding me back from my past, allowing me to start growing and developing into who I was meant to become.

This phase of my life was the kickstart of my passion for understanding people: how we work, what derails progress, and what maximizes our growth. I spent over a year searching to understand who I was and how I work: the good, the bad, and the extreme. This was not a surface-level overview but a deep dive into what had led me to make certain decisions or choose specific pathways.

Take a moment to consider anything that you are passionate about or good at. How many hours have you invested in that subject matter or expertise? Then consider other things in your life and think about how many hours you have spent running down the rabbit trail of each new passion. The issue I know you will find, just as I did, is that we spend so many hours learning and studying things that interest us or that we are passionate about, but we spend minimal time studying who we are and what we are built to take on.

Canadian journalist and author Malcolm Gladwell wrote, *"It takes ten thousand hours to truly master anything. Time spent leads to experience; experience leads to proficiency; and the more proficient you are, the more valuable you'll be."* What if you and I spent this much time focusing on how best to live our lives and act in alignment with who we are and our greatest skills? How much further could each of us be if we created the discipline to connect to the core foundations of ourselves?

When was the last time you went down a spiral, getting a bit nerdy on the inner workings of the way your brain is programmed or details of the skills and natural bends that are within your God-given abilities? Neither the school system nor most parents teach us how to use the greatest tool we have ever been given: who we are at our core.

This is a fundamental issue for most people and was a major problem in the earlier phase of my life. I am nowhere near the ten-thousand-hour rule for becoming an expert on myself, but I am constantly learning, growing, and connecting with the core aspects of who I am and what drives, influences, and holds me back.

Many people are driven to these kinds of understandings on the backside of failure or patterns of mistakes, but what if we focused on these matters out of sheer desire for our growth, development, and maximum momentum? How much greater could the results become? How much more ground could be covered on the road to success? How many failures and mistakes could be avoided?

I am not asking you to sit and stare in the mirror, memorizing every aspect of your appearance; I'm asking you to go deeper. I highly recommend taking the time to start with a few different personality tests, such as the DISC (a tool that assesses behavior and communication styles) and the Enneagram (which categorizes personality types based on motivations and fears). Try a few career tests, not for career searching, but use them for the personality profiles and details of the results. I will add a link to a great platform on the resources page that offers many options. I also recommend using cognitive tests, which can help you understand how your brain processes information and how you problem-solve.

The results of each one listed above shouldn't be reviewed in a surface-level aspect, but rather, they should be used to identify how the strengths have shown up in your past so you can clearly see any areas of weakness you operate in. I still retake personality tests that I took in my early twenties to keep learning how to maximize my output. The goal is to define and sharpen your "edge": the top 20 percent of all your skill sets, capabilities, and abilities. This will enable you to live at your highest level of output with every ounce of energy you expend.

Understanding who you are is about really connecting with the areas you should focus on and the areas you need to avoid. Depending on your position or role in the organization, or if you are a CEO or entrepreneur, the key takeaways from your discovery may be to initially identify areas you should delegate immediately. As you dig deeper into your understanding and connect to the core of you, there is a freeing aspect to assigning the projects and tasks within your range of weaknesses to someone who fits the strengths needed.

This isn't a book focused on team building, leadership, or delegation, but a quick leadership tip is understanding yourself and then fully understanding each team member's edge. Then teach your team to leverage their output by focusing on the top 20 percent of activities that move the needle and build the most momentum. This all starts with you and understanding how to connect to your core and maximize your own output.

Once you work through a process like this and can differentiate who you are and the skill sets you have from prior programming and others' expectations, you can start to set expectations built on truth. The most important aspect is to approach this with curiosity and exploration, work to fully understand yourself, and challenge everything you once knew based on your prior programming.

The issue I have found is that all the planning and long-term goals based on faulty information are prone to major errors and failures along the way. This is why the reality check we all need is to step back and gain a full understanding of who we are, without the pre-programmed aspects and expectations from our childhoods.

Create Your Display

The process broken down above is not just here to keep you busy but rather to give you the right tools and knowledge to execute appropriate planning. This is about bringing to light your greatest attributes and giving you clarity on the areas where you need to focus your efforts.

I like to connect this next part of the process to a trophy display cabinet. Take a second and think about the purpose of the trophy display cabinet: to draw attention to the greatness of the trophies inside. We should create our own "trophy display" for ourselves for our planning and execution.

Step back from the fact that all the test results from the previous process belong to you and focus on analyzing and highlighting the most significant aspects of the data. Allow yourself to celebrate all the great parts of who you are and the skill sets, abilities, and best attributes that are fundamental to your core.

I have worked with people who really struggle to accept their strengths and only focus on their weaknesses. In these situations, it is important to print and remove any pages or sections that discuss weaknesses or areas of lesser greatness. This moment is about accepting and highlighting the areas where you shine.

Once you have fully connected to all the areas of strengths and abilities, there needs to be a process for identifying the greatest capabilities that could emerge if they were driven by the right fuel and executed with the right focus. This isn't just about acknowledging who you are today, but identifying what you are capable of becoming with who you were built to be.

When I worked through all of this in my own life, I realized that all my goals and ambitions had been set with too many limitations. Once I took a step back and focused only on the strengths and skill sets on paper, not through the lens of my past, programming, or others' expectations, I was able to see the full potential of who I was built to become.

One of my clients came to me and told me he didn't feel "worthy" or good enough to achieve the goals he was setting. I explained the good news is that, right now, he wasn't capable of achieving the massive goals he was setting for the next ten or twenty years. He hadn't yet done the work to achieve those outcomes. This process is about understanding what you are capable of if you focus your everyday attention on maximizing the output and development of your strengths.

This is all about connecting to the compounding effect of your daily disciplines and habits with focused attention on leveraging your strengths. New York Times Best-Selling Author James Clear breaks this down: *"Habits are the compound interest of self-improvement. The same way that money multiplies through compound interest, the effects of your habits multiply as you repeat them."*

The problem is that most people's goals and ambitions are based on comparisons with others, the expectations placed on them, or the beliefs instilled in them. The compounding effect will only reach its maximum potential if your daily habits align with who you truly are and the great outcomes you are built to achieve.

The version you display should reflect the best aspects of your development and progress. Your strengths and most impactful attributes should be detailed and developed over the years in ways that impact your life's momentum and goals. The display should focus on what you could become if you develop your areas of greatness and natural gifts. Only after you set a clear display for yourself will the truth of what you are capable of achieving become clear. This will require focused effort to develop your strengths and deploy yourself in the areas you are built to pursue.

The clarity required in this process makes it vital to remove distractions and confront the root source: your cracked lenses. The programming inside us can derail our progress and our understanding of who we are. Taking the time to learn how we are built is right at our fingertips.

My hope for you is that you begin the process of becoming an expert in who you are and what you are capable of achieving. The ten-thousand-hour rule might seem a little extreme, but taking a deep dive into yourself and engaging in internal reflection will be time well spent. Only when you confront what you previously knew and go through a new process of self-identification and understanding will you have the expertise to lay the foundation for your future.

Revisit Your Dreams

Leonardo da Vinci laid the foundation for all of us to build on with his statement, *"I have been impressed with the urgency of doing. Knowing is not enough; we must apply. Being willing is not enough; we must do."* This phase of your journey is not just about gaining new knowledge and understanding but about incorporating these developments into your actions. Yes, the process of connecting to the core fundamentals of who you are and clearly identifying your display is powerful, but revisiting your dreams is a required next step.

In Chapter Two, I talked about three types of dreams, and as you implement awareness of a new, displayed version of yourself, I implore you to push hard into the dreams you never knew could be yours. With this new understanding of how your skill sets and abilities could develop, you need to recast your ideals of what your outcomes could be.

When you take the time to lay out the action steps and fully connect with the development possible for the person you were built to become, it can ignite dream-casting. The way this worked for me was unlocking new levels I never knew were within my reach. The dreams I had to focus on were ones I thought were only for specific people, like those with specific upbringings or financial statuses. I knew that once I was fully connected to the best version of myself, I could see my future differently.

The goals I set for myself and the dreams I laid out for my future were ones the prior version of me would have only laughed at and never seriously considered. The process I went through, as I laid out above, was the start of clarity of vision and a connection to a whole new level of potential. Working backward and revisiting the dreams you have set for your life after you create the version of yourself reflected in the mirror is a safety net that helps minimize the risk of major regrets.

The new actions, informed by new knowledge and information about who you are, should start challenging what was once set in place as the dreams you are chasing. Here are some focused reflections that can assist in your process:

- What fears or hesitations have I taken into my dreams?
- What cracked lenses about who I am, what I am capable of, or what my future could become might be present in my dream casting?
- Have I fully connected with my greatest strengths and defined the version of myself I display?
- What is the greatest development and growth I could create through the right daily disciplines and maximizing my greatest abilities?
- What could my life really look like if I let go of my insecurities and areas of life that held me back and chased wholeheartedly after the person I was built to become?
- What dreams can I lay out for my life that I didn't know could be mine?

The Line in the Sand

This is the point, the line in the sand, where there are no more excuses for not having a clear roadmap to connect to your potential. I am dedicated to supporting people and even laying this out so everyone has the keys to open the door to their best future success. I cannot control what you do with it, but the process outlined above has completely changed my life and significantly impacted the people and teams I work with.

I understand that some might want or need help working through this entire process. Also, I find that having a coach who guides you helps you make the most of the process. This is one of the areas where my team and I can be of service. On the resources page, you will find contact information to schedule a discovery call with my team if you feel you or your team needs support on this journey.

I cannot stress enough how important this chapter and process are to your success and the future opportunities you can create. I didn't have someone provide me with a roadmap or layout for this process; I had to stumble through it alone and steer the course of my life.

I have come to realize that anything I learn deepens my understanding and is something I can never unlearn. This is what I want to do for you: give you all of this so you can never unlearn this information and the opportunity it can bring to your future. This is exactly why I have laid all of this out and given you my personal story as a testament to the process. Yes, you have decisions to make and a crossroads to face about what to do with this information, but now you know where to start to create a greater future.

CHAPTER 7

Control the Tides

I believe in honesty, and as a leader of many, I am not one to keep secrets. This is why, as I am leading you through the important aspects we have covered and will continue to cover together, I need to be completely open and vulnerable about something in my life: I have found enjoyment, laughter, and even comfort in others' hardships and failures. Many times, I replay their failures or watch in great anticipation to see how they will handle themselves and make even greater mistakes. Watching the domino effect of miscalculated steps and knee-jerk reactions leading to unthinkable outcomes is humorous and entertaining to me.

I know you might be thinking, *What a sick dude*, but let me explain what I am talking about. See, there are some great social media channels I often watch. Many of these channels focus on the challenges faced by boat captains, particularly regarding boat ramps and inlet waterways.

This might not sound very amusing to you, but before you cast judgment on me, make sure you take a few minutes and Google "boat captain fails." I am sure it will pull up many channels, such as The Qualified Captain, Ramp Champs, Boating Fails, and many others, with an almost unlimited supply of videos. If you have never driven a boat through saltwater channels and inlets or, most importantly, attempted to trailer a boat during shifting tides, you are missing out.

I came across one of these channels years ago while searching for tips on the best ways to manage my boat's trailering during shifting tides, and I became hooked. This discovery immediately made me feel so much better about the difficulty I had one Saturday getting my boat back on the trailer. I dealt with a flood of frustration and had to ignore the humiliation I felt during the attempt and the prior failed attempts. Just knowing that others had failed even more than I had normalized the issue for me, and now I can just laugh at it.

The ability to manage docking a boat is not easy for many people, especially when you consider the movement of tides and the need to calculate drift, which affects the front (the bow) of your boat differently from the back (the stern). (I added in the technical terms because if I didn't, I would have avid boaters or captains reading this book getting a little squirrelly on me.)

For those who have never experienced the hardships discussed above, make sure you at least watch a few videos to get a sense of the full measure of humility that comes with such situations. As a captain, there are so many aspects to consider when running a boat. I don't want to talk down to freshwater captains, but the salt-life game adds so many more levels of complexity. Navigating the tides, the flow of currents in the inlets, and all the channel markers when you're on the water with the other boaters who are unprepared and undertrained for the waterways adds a bit of stress to the environment.

For me, the enjoyment of watching these boaters' struggles and failures comes from the fact that their only real risk is a bit of damage to the boat, yet it's a big hit to their pride. I can laugh at their struggles because I can relate to their pain and frustration. On the other hand, I would never laugh at the expense of others when I see them struggling in major areas of life similar to the difficult ones I've experienced. I think the major difference is the magnitude of what is at stake. There is a sobering reality when the risk escalates or the potential for hurt and failure increases due to missteps or wrong adjustments.

The tides of the ocean are destined to change, and at each point, the effects on your vessel will differ. Whether you're on the water or trying to dock or trailer the boat, it's vital to know what difficulties you'll deal with. Skills need to be developed, and running a boat is an art to be learned. Being aware of all these moving pieces and forces that shift your vessel and create navigational difficulties is essential to the journey.

This is very similar to where you are in your journey through this book and in your life at this moment. You must recognize the tides in your life and how they affect your path. Understanding the tides in life that you have faced and will continue to face is very important. Without that awareness, the tides will inevitably push you off course.

It is not just about putting your head down and pushing forward toward the version of you that you have set for yourself and the goals, dreams, and ambitions you are capable of achieving. You have to acknowledge the push and pull of the tides and be aware that course corrections may be necessary to maintain control despite them.

The Push, The Pull

The tides are at work all around us, attempting to push and pull us in different directions. Some are easy to recognize, while others are silent killers we never see coming. The awareness of these tides allows you to control their effects on your development and even your decision-making.

An endless number of tides could be present, but I find it important to dive into some of them to raise your awareness and ability to identify them and others in your life. As we look at the different tides that could be present in your life, there are two areas to separate them into: the external and the internal. While these may vary for each of us, both are vital to keep under active monitoring, ensuring your vessel maintains a navigational direction aligned with the future you are intentionally building.

External factors can be widespread, and discernment is required when considering conversations, relationships, opportunities, and other factors. I've encountered what seemed like incredible opportunities throughout my life. However, after employing my discernment process to check their alignment with the "lighthouse" I've established for my life, I've had to recognize them for what they truly are: distractions or strong currents of distraction that could potentially pull me off course.

The same goes for relationships; you have to have a high level of discernment, not only to identify whether the person will contribute to growth, accountability, or support for the journey, but also to see if they will derail the progress required for it. The difficult part of relationships comes from those perceived as foundational, such as family, or from those that have been in our lives since childhood or for long periods of time. This is where granular-level discernment needs to be interlaced into every conversation.

Many people in our lives don't understand the mission we have chosen for ourselves. They might not understand your goals and what you have implemented for the long-term outcomes you are chasing. This can become an issue because they might even have great intentions, but they can be a shifting tide you're not ready to counter.

To go even further, expectations are often put on us by those we have known for longer seasons; they have expectations for what we should do with our lives and what they feel our success should look like, even to the point of how we show up in specific situations. This can be a major push or pull for each of us, as many of those relationships are with loved ones or people who have supported us through difficult seasons.

To turn this boat in a slightly more difficult direction, there are people who are out to get things from us and may never admit it, but they want things for our lives so they can benefit from us. This could also be based on how your accomplishments or specific results would make them feel about themselves. These are areas where having a solid foundation for what the displayed version of you should look like and the goals and ambitions you are built to take on creates a bar to compare everything against. Those direct relationships can be very difficult to navigate and set proper boundaries around when needed. This is why awareness and recognition are vital; you have to be able to identify those people who are actually in your corner, supporting your growth and true development.

Take a moment and consider the difficulty connected to navigating a waterway, like an inlet or a canal, that has shifting tides, currents, and all the navigational markers that are there to keep you from running onto shallow waters or rocks. Think about all the preparation you would have done, all the hours spent being challenged, and the captain's skills you might bring into that circumstance. How fast could this situation worsen if five other boats attempted the same navigation, but their captains were unprepared and lacked the processing and problem-solving skills that you have? Think about the journey you are on and the people around you. Are you being distracted by their actions, steps, and journeys? These can become major noise in your life, distracting you from the focus that needs your undivided attention.

I am not saying that you cannot support others, but remember, we are trained to always put on our own oxygen mask before attempting to help others. Take this time in your life to pave your path, find your greatness, and be defined by who you are and what you are chasing after before you assist others around you. The floundering of others on their path may derail your journey if you let it.

External factors are not just limited to relationships; the list of sources from which tides stem from could be endless. The most important aspect is identifying areas of your life where you have allowed tides to move you. Social media is a major source of pushing and pulling against the direction many of my clients are headed, allowing the influence of this noise to become a distraction that shapes their vision of their life. With the attention-seeking aspects of social media, it isn't about truth or even what is best for those watching, but rather gaining attention and influencing others to take action.

This becomes the undercurrent that can sneak up on you when you least expect it. You scroll through social media and hear all the messages of what it looks like to be successful; you hear others' claimed stories of their results, and you start the comparison game. You see the life others claim to live and the picture of perfection they want you to believe. This is one of the biggest dream-destroyers I have ever seen. People give up on their journey because they see others getting results faster or with less effort, which can be disheartening.

I have seen firsthand the claims of my former clients in my prior business in which they stated they had hit specific growth or revenue targets, but in fact, the claims were not correct. This has been a constant issue. Never believe what is said on social media unless their claims can be substantiated. Then, most importantly, never compare your journey to theirs, even if their results are true.

I have seen people give up on their dreams because of lies told online, and people believed them. Social media and so many other sources have become an outlet for a dopamine hit from the biggest lie or false reality someone can claim and get attention for. This is a shame, as all too many people are hit by a tide that compares them to false claims, and they struggle on their journey because of it. Also take into consideration the standard economic, cultural, political, and religious pressures that come into play in each of our lives: what may be expected of us because of where we were raised, the color of our skin, our physical appearance, or any other factors. These are all "tides" that create potential movements that derail us off course if we are not aware and ready to counter-navigate.

These external factors can sometimes feel like they are pulling us in multiple directions. Although I've only listed a few examples for you, reflect on your own life to identify ones that resonate with you. As you continue moving forward, it is also important to use these examples to increase your awareness and discern how they can show up and affect your momentum. This, combined with your clear understanding of the displayed version of you, gives you clarity and a bar to measure everything against.

I strongly recommend that you make a list of factors you can identify that could create or influence external tides in your life. List them out specifically and what the effects would be of each if you do not manage them and course-correct. I also highly recommend you create a list of identifiers for when these are present, which might be specific actions or a lack of actions that you need to hold yourself accountable for.

Early in this book, we covered the definition of what I call "cracked lenses." These are the biggest sources of "internal tides" that will create the push or the pull and get you off navigational track. I would not even be able to count the number of times I have taken my focus off of how my cracked lenses allowed me to slowly drift. There are many aspects of my past, my childhood, past relationships, experiences, and traumas I have been through, and many other factors that affect how I see myself and what I am capable of.

It requires a dedicated focus to seal the cracks in our lenses so we can see ourselves at our fullest potential. The truth is, these cracks don't vanish overnight. Healing them requires a consistent new way of framing your experiences, one that gradually shifts how they impact your life today and your vision for tomorrow. Not allowing them to derail us requires dedication and, during some seasons, daily focus and attention.

The internal tides at play in your life could be as simple as fears and insecurities that hold you back or pull you toward a safer route. For some people, fears and insecurities are the default way they have viewed circumstances and the expectations for outcomes. This is where, as we discussed in Chapter Three, the importance of challenging everything and diving into the root causes, using the tool "the inner two-year-old," which requires you to look deeper into the why behind each internal tide that is steering you off course.

I used my own life as an example of these tides, noting my tendency to stay in the shadows due to childhood experiences with my older brother. I had to figure out why the fear of being the center of attention existed. Whenever I became the center of attention, insecurities seemed to flood my mind and become almost crippling. My brother had a tendency to steal the spotlight whenever I was the center of attention. These situations normally ended with him mocking me, picking on my weight or other deficits in his eyes, and embarrassing me in front of my friends or peer groups.

The tides that are inside of you that could be pushing or pulling you in other directions could be based on the guidance you received throughout your childhood: the things that you were "strongly encouraged" to do and the expectations that were put on you to go a specific direction with your career or education.

Also, the things we heard in childhood about finances and even religion may have created parameters that often cause our minds to automatically bend or be drawn in specific directions. You must recognize these tides within you and understand your stance on them, not just because they were engraved in you, but because understanding them will help you determine your true beliefs.

The awareness needed about your internal tides is vital, as they can stem from almost any area. Perhaps when you were growing up, you watched someone you looked up to climb their success ladder, and now the bar you have set for yourself isn't based on your journey or what your success could look like but on theirs and their life.

The issue for most of us is that we are taught and trained from a young age to listen, learn, and follow directions. The school system and the corporate ladder are built on thriving within parameters set by others, according to their definition of success and acceptable outcomes.

I will be completely honest: I did not do well at falling into the mold required by the school system, which is why I am forever grateful to my parents for taking the time to customize my learning experience throughout my younger years. They focused on celebrating my specific strengths, not making me feel ashamed for my areas of weakness. That would have been crippling, given the expectations of the school system.

Through the struggle and fight to study and grow, I have taken the time to uncover, learn, and leverage the way my brain processes, and I've turned what others may call a disadvantage into my refined superpower. These labels given to you may be tides pulling or pushing you and derailing your progress. I understand that it is difficult to reframe everything you might have heard, and even the excuses you have been given, but this is your life, your story, and your one opportunity to create greatness, and nothing others put on you should hold you back. This is why it's important to reflect on these types of situations in your history and identify how they are impacting your story.

You may have past relationships that have created incredible scar tissue, damaging your programming and even making you feel less than or never good enough. The pain from your past and the deep cuts of hurt can never be taken back, but you need to choose if you are going to allow them to control your path. I am not just talking about romantic relationships here, but also close friendships, relatives, and direct family relationships.

These tides are strong, and the currents they create will derail your progress unless you work through properly reframing them to stop allowing them to shift your direction. This requires a lot of inner work and even a daily reframing of the past to remove the power they hold over your life. This is not easy, but this is one of the most important pieces you need to get under control.

You must direct how you allow the past to influence today and every day thereafter, even though the past will never change. Although someone in your past caused these internal tides, you must take action to limit the destruction. You cannot allow them to cripple the displayed version of you and how you are showing up. If this hits close to home in your situation and you struggle with allowing these situations in your life, I strongly recommend you work back through Chapter Five and reach out to my team.

The connection, identification, and awareness of our tides that push and pull us are major parts of our growth and development. Many intrinsic factors are at play that trigger automatic responses, reactions, and heuristics, which could drive us to actions that are not in line with the goals we set. Each and every one of your moves matters, and the navigation required must take into consideration the tides that come from both internal and external factors.

Tides from Our Self-Inflicted Wounds

If you feel haunted by your past, it may create additional internal and external tides, depending on the situations that have occurred. Our past may cause self-inflicted wounds, past mistakes, unresolved issues, failures, and even the relationships that we have been on the destructive side of. Each of these has its own connective tissue that seems to hold us in place as we attempt to move forward in our lives. They can be tides or currents that pull us, push us, or even, at times, seem like ghost pirate ships that attack us out of nowhere.

Some of us may feel stuck in a cycle of failure we cannot escape. It feels as though no matter what we accomplish and the success we achieve, we don't deserve the rewards. The outcomes feel too good to be true, and we self-destruct. For other people, actual consequences arise from how they have handled situations or the reputations they have built. Some let past failures haunt them, and fear of repeating them paralyzes their actions.

Even though each of us has elements of our lives that tend to bring up regrets, shame, frustration, fear, and insecurities, we have to connect to the raw truth that these things will not define us. What are those things in your life that could be creating these tides or driving the currents that could derail your progress? We all carry the past into each day we face, and it is always based on what has happened before this moment.

This is not only about the bad things; we also carry the burden from our greatest successes and past progress. The pressure to maintain our high performance can be daily, and the mental expectations we place on ourselves can lead to major derailment. Everyone has the past stepping on their heels, and some feel the need to supersede their last greatest moment, while others need to prove they have overcome their mistakes and failures.

My encouragement for you is that what defines you is who you choose to be on a daily basis moving forward. Yes, you might have royally screwed up in the past and even failed in ways that make you feel you don't deserve a better future. Some of the best stories of hope are those in which the early parts have hardships, failures, and even massive regrets, but there was recovery, reconciliation, and a complete change that allowed for greatness to shine.

The most important aspect is what you do with everything you have learned and grown from and the knowledge you have accumulated, taking greater action than what your past may have been filled with. This is the compounding effect of taking lessons from failure, difficulty, and success and applying them to the next step or mission. You might have a rough past or even a traumatic story of failures and mistakes, but these are not what define you.

Take steps daily to show up in a new way and maximize all the lessons you have learned to create a greater future than anyone could imagine for your life. Don't allow the shifting tides to decide your outcome; the reality that you choose to live in, with the displayed version of you as the guide, provides a new definition of who you are and the outcome of the story you will live.

They Don't Get to Decide

With the weight of this chapter and the broached subject matters, I feel it necessary to reassure you that the people from your past and even those people who are currently in your life don't get to decide the outcome of your story. They are not the author, nor do they control how your days are spent.

I know it is tough, as it is easy to let people from your past and the expectations placed on you be the motivating and directional factors. In some situations, there might even be people you feel you have failed so badly that it would only enrage them further to see you succeed. If they choose to feel that way, there's nothing you can do about it, and the great news is that it is not up to them how you chase after your future. There are some situations where it might be best to go back and seek a resolution or ask for forgiveness, but you cannot control the other person's response or reaction.

In the journey of working to become the greatest version of yourself, there are many things that might be required of you, and I guarantee many of them will be awkward and uncomfortable. I have found that the more I strive to become a better version of myself, the more I have to swallow my pride, be open to criticism, and do the hard things that others may not be aligned with. The responsibility is completely on you to take steps each day with the gifts, strengths, and greatness that have been entrusted to you.

I have had to go back and apologize for how I have handled things in my past; just ask my kids. I am not always the most incredible parent, but I am constantly pushing to learn, grow, and develop in every way. Now that my daughter is an adult, she and I have had some tough conversations about how we navigated a very difficult time in our lives. I told her that I did the best with what I knew at the time and was constantly working to parent my best with the tools I had at my fingertips. The truth is, there are countless things I could have handled better with her.

The same is true with my son. He is not shocked when I go back to him and say, "I am not sure why I just said no; that was just my initial reaction," or "Man, I am just trying to figure this whole parenting thing out, dealing with each situation we face and doing my best given all we have had to deal with."

This being said, I am sure there are failures or mistakes I made that they might have issues with or resentments against me for later in life. This will not stop my mission or vision, nor will it change my constant move toward a better me and my life because of their feelings from the past. They don't get to decide. I do.

I have asked for forgiveness and moved to become better, but if their resentments eat at them and they don't truly forgive me, that is on them. I can only control how I handle myself, how I react to each situation, and how I manage my failures. This is why we have to connect to all the aspects of the waterways we have navigated and the people who have been involved in our lives. We always have to maintain our own perspective and focus on our lighthouse, despite feelings or reactions from others. You must remain in full control of each step of your own journey.

Guess what? We all have people in our past; some haunt us in our regrets, and others are a part of our hurts. Some have set expectations for us, and some have been a major source of cracks in our lenses. Those whom we have wanted approval from, and others we have wanted to be good enough to be accepted by. None of these people decide the future that you will live or the person you can become. Their thoughts, approval, acceptance, and opinions don't matter.

Steve Jobs, Co-founder of Apple, Creator of Pixar Studios, and known as a leading Visionary Entrepreneur, once said, *"Your time is limited, so don't waste it living someone else's life."* You are the one in control of your story and how each day is written on those pages, and you get to create the entire storyline from this day until your last breath. This life is your own; other people can live their own lives and walk out their own paths, but they can never dictate how yours is to be lived. None of these individuals will be lying on your deathbed with you, personally accounting for how you have managed your life, made the best of your opportunities, and chased after your dreams.

I understand this is easier said than actually done, but I need you to take ownership as the only one who gets to decide what your life will become.

What Kind of "Safe" Are You Living In?

Taking the time to work through all of these concepts in this chapter can be very difficult, and I am not assuming this is a "fly" chapter; you know, those chapters in books that are surface-level and you can cruise through without emotion or creating action steps in your life. This is one of those I would deem a bit tough, with aspects that you might even say are rather uncomfortable. I am perfectly happy taking you through processes that are uncomfortable and stretch you outside your comfort zone. Growth, development, and, I would even argue, success have never been found within one's comfort zone. The type of life that you are chasing after and that you are capable of requires you to get uncomfortable, outside of what you may consider safe.

This is why I need you to take some time here at the end of this already tough chapter and reflect on the "safe" you are living in or drawn to. This is another tide that can be shifting your course or navigation on your voyage. It may also be the fact that you are completely failing yourself by setting your destination completely wrong. You might have too much focus on safety and security rather than on the adventure you were built to take on in your lifetime.

It might be a great exercise for you to connect with the most successful people you can and ask whether their goals and ambitions were ever in danger. Maybe you have lost sight of what safety looks like, but if the goals that you set don't make you a bit nervous, they are probably not big enough.

I put checks and balances in place in my life: if the person I am today is capable of achieving my goals, then my goals are not extravagant enough. The goals, visions, and missions that I set out to achieve all must require a "greater Nate Green" than who I am today. They all require heavy growth, development, and learning new skills to accomplish them.

So, I ask you, what "safe" are you living in? Why are you not getting outside of your comfort zone? I know it would be nice to live in safety and security while reaching your full potential, but that is just not how it works. An impactful quote that brings this into perspective is from poet T. S. Eliot: *"Only those who will risk going too far can possibly find out how far one can go."*

There is an extreme truth about each and every one of us being programmed to seek safety and security as part of the ingrained nature of humanity, but we have to move toward a higher risk tolerance to identify our true potential. You are built to take on challenges and grow to be able to conquer new feats. Your life needs the best version of you to face the challenges ahead.

The outcomes you set as your greatest goals require you to get uncomfortable, take risks, and break through the obstacles that have been holding you back. There are no shortcuts to success, and there are no golden tickets that allow you to bypass the risk factors. "Safe" should never be the focus; the future you can create should be your guide.

Your Lighthouse as Your Guide

In the shifting waterways of life, movement without a destination is simply a slow drift toward derailment. To stay the course, you must establish a lighthouse, a fixed pillar that keeps you aligned even when the internal and external tides pull hardest. This isn't just about what you want to achieve; it's about the foundation of who you are becoming. By layering the displayed version of your greatest potential into this framework, you create a beacon that pierces through the fog of your past hardships and even the distractions of your current success. Your passions, your purpose, and your legacy must all intersect here. With a defined lighthouse, the cracks in your lenses no longer dictate the direction, and the tides lose their ability to derail your progress.

Your lighthouse should not be easy to achieve but rather filled with what I consider deathbed goals, ambitions, and legacy. This requires you to go beyond any comfort and security, think far beyond what you are currently capable of achieving, and cast a vision for the most incredible achievements you could hope to accomplish in your lifetime.

There are so many aspects to cover when it comes to what I consider to be one's lighthouse. In my prior book, *Suck Less, Do Better*, I dive into many aspects of this in the chapter titled "Set Your Lighthouse." If you have not read that book, I highly recommend it, as I push hard into fundamentals that I feel are vital for everyone to understand as they are creating the definition of their success journey.

If you don't focus on your goals, life's ups and downs will throw you off course. Creating a clear lighthouse for your life helps you always keep the end in mind as you face any storm or difficulty. This provides directional focus, allowing you to weigh opportunities and even relationships to determine whether they align with the direction for your life.

I utilize my lighthouse to determine and set a navigation course, which ensures I will create the catalyst for my growth. I am just like most entrepreneurial people; my guess is that you are as well, and if we do not have some boundaries or parameters in place, we get distracted by the shiny objects that cross our paths. The lighthouse in my life is a guide to determine whether opportunities or potential are in line with the person I am striving to become, the impact I am dedicated to making, and the purpose for which I want my life to be built.

Implementing a long-term guide provides clarity, vision, and a destination for our actions to align with. Are there seasons when updates have to be made to redirect you toward your lighthouse? Of course. Having the light during moments of darkness, a bar for comparison when distracted, will be the catalyst you need as you push forward in the difficult moments on the journey.

The truth we must face is that the tides are shifting, and the only decision is how you will allow them to affect your growth, development, and future outcomes. You must commit to the difficult work in the areas where you are being intrinsically derailed. This requires two things: first, you'll need to set necessary boundaries with those around you who may be influencing your direction; and second, you must reflect on the areas of your life where you caused the currents and tides that shift your movements.

As I have discussed, this chapter carries significant weight. These core fundamentals are the hidden currents and tides that quietly derail high-potential people, pulling them away from the greatness they were meant to achieve. While confronting these areas is a requirement for growth, the work of identification and the correction of the drift must start with you.

My responsibility is to lay the foundation and provide the principles you need to control the tides and build your momentum, but I cannot sail the ship for you. You must take full ownership of the story you are writing and the direction you are heading. There is a far greater outcome waiting for you, but reaching it requires more than just interest; it demands your active, eager, and relentless participation.

CHAPTER 8

Fill the Tank

"Your drive and hunger remind me of middle school relationships," I said to James as we sat with each other, looking over his last ten years of entrepreneurship. "They are quick to ignite and then fast to burn out, leaving a bit of destruction. Could you share what remains from all the efforts and successes you've mentioned?"

He struggled to explain that, right now, he was financially broke but had learned strategies he could take into his next launch. I said to him, "The 'broke' part is a tough pill to swallow, and it's great to leverage the lessons and strategies, but how will you ensure you don't have the same end result in another ten years?"

James wasn't able to explain how he could create a different outcome, and he frustratedly said, "That is why I hired you. I need to be fixed."

I asked James to paint a picture of what the success he had been chasing would look like in ten, twenty, and thirty years. The way he explained it clearly to me was shocking, as it was much different from his actions. We worked together to identify where his stated goals and ambitions were a complete mismatch with his last ten years of effort.

I explained to him that you can set goals and have an incredibly painted "lighthouse" for your life, but if you are not honest with yourself about what is driving you, the likelihood of derailment is high. The issue is that most of us have the motivation to propel us to take action, but in many cases, these motivators drive us toward conflicting outcomes. The most reasonable part of us cognitively connects to long-term goals and ambitions, including why we are pursuing those directions, but internal drivers from other factors can create a whirlwind of emotions that push us to take different actions.

The life that James had lived included some tough seasons; some might say that he was a bit of a "tough cookie." His rebellious spirit and the way he communicated didn't get him many brownie points with those in authority over him or his peers. This placed him in an outsider role in his school and constantly put him in trouble with the leadership team and his parents.

He broke down. He told me that what pushed him further down this path was constantly being told he needed to be like other people. The bar of expectation was set to make him feel less than, and the others who were thriving in specific areas became the standard. One moment he felt heartbreak was when his parents made a list of other kids in his community, detailing their strengths, creating the perfect kid on paper, and then telling him he needed to strive to become like that.

Yes, James was a handful, but no one took the time to understand who he was or what made him great. Rather, they were constantly forcing him to conform to global standards and expectations. This was compounded by the ongoing mockery from those around him and the jabs from his siblings, who seemed to have fallen in line. The messages that he heard directly or indirectly were "You will never be good enough," "You aren't acceptable as you are," "You are going to fail and never be a success," and "You are only acceptable when you are succeeding." So he developed a habit of comparing himself to others and their strengths. This was an equation for the massive cracks in his lenses through which he viewed himself: *Let's create the picture of the perfect person, pieced together by everyone else's strengths, and then compare myself to them.*

These messages, which drilled deeply into his psychological programming, showed up later in his life and were part of the cycle of derailment he was experiencing. This pain point that he was dealing with is known as one of the five in Maslow's Hierarchy of Needs: *"Love and belongingness reflects the human need for social connection, including friendship, family, and romantic relationships. A sense of belonging and acceptance is essential for psychological well-being and can even override safety needs in some cases."*

Even though James had matured in many ways, this programming was still deep inside him, driving him to take actions and make specific decisions. Let me land the plane by explaining that ten years ago, James' two main fuel sources became his cracked childhood lenses and his more mature sense of purpose.

He defaulted to what most of us do: the need for acceptance. Even Maslow breaks down the fact that the demand for love and belonging, including acceptance, can be so strong that some would even ignore the need for safety in order to obtain them. It's why James was defaulting to fulfill this need in his life more than the fuel connected to his long-term purpose and goals.

James was playing out a cycle of diving headlong into a business or sales role. He would push hard and give his maximum effort, and as a result, he would find killer results that others would identify, acknowledge, and celebrate. This would then fulfill the need that he was striving for, so he would lean in and become the life of the party. During this phase of the cycle, he would pay for others to join him for dinner, drinks, and other activities. This would also drive his purchasing habits, and it would always be based upon the group at the time and what they deemed as success.

One time, he purchased a motorcycle. Another time, it was a Maserati, and right before our meeting, it was a Ferrari. The result was always the same: he would push on the brakes of his goals so he could gain the acceptance that came with each group's support and camaraderie. This need drove James to extreme lengths. His initial dedication to achieving results led to the destruction of his success and the depletion of all financial gains he had earned. Any support, celebration, and results-based praise faded as he squandered his money and opportunities, leading him back to the point where he had to start over.

Here was the cycle: he would hit rock bottom, develop his next plan or success mission, and then begin deploying maximum effort again. He had some insight into his long-term goals, but the need for acceptance, to be celebrated, supported, and a part of the group, would take over and pull him back into his cycle.

Even if you think you would stay on track, the reality is that the deep-rooted programming in each of us creates drivers that can take us off the path we're supposed to be on. That is the reason why the last chapter was broken down into so much detail to help you connect to the tides in your life that could be derailing your navigation.

Each one of us has to be cautious about the fuel we allow to fill our tanks and the leverage we use to keep us driven and motivated on the journey. The life you have lived up to this moment might not be as extreme as James's, but I can guarantee that there are things programmed into you that have created cracked lenses distorting what your success looks like.

Or maybe your parents were perfect, and you have no scars from your relationships. If that is the case, I would strongly recommend you ask your parents to write a playbook for the rest of us parents. I know it would be extremely helpful, as many of us are doing the best we can, one day at a time. Yes, I know sarcasm doesn't resonate with everyone, but I can't help myself when discussing these critically important areas. Some people aren't willing to do the hard work of reflecting on and uncovering these realities in their lives.

The reason I tell you all about these stories is to help you understand you are not alone. The reason I know these cracks must be identified and overcome is that I've lived the consequences of not confronting them. I cannot stress this enough: cracked lenses will breed broken dreams in your life. It is not just a book title; it is the raw truth.

I have seen this firsthand and watched as people resisted working through their past and charged forward in their lives, only to find consistent failure. I have worked with others who are driven to acknowledge and overcome their cracked lenses, and this allows for focused momentum and incredible outcomes. Momentum can be built on the other side of understanding these core issues, and helping you succeed is where my passion lies.

Each principle within this book is here for a purpose; I am not about adding any fluff for entertainment or page count. My hope for you is that you take each aspect and element seriously and apply them to your life. As you build momentum, focus on the fuel systems you can use and those that may distract or destroy your ability to achieve your goals.

Cracks Create Distracting Fuel

The reflection process is difficult because much of what is deeply rooted in us may be normalized and just part of what we know. This is why I want to point out that, as in James's situation, your life might have distractions, and using the wrong source of fuel can lead to cracked lenses in the long run.

Take the time to do a detailed check of the fuel that is driving you. What fuel in your tank keeps you moving forward? What are the detailed goals, ambitions, and outcomes that you are striving for? You must also consider the hidden drivers of success that you haven't fully connected to. Are there any cycles present that are driving you toward failure? Are you drawn toward any actions that could destroy those goals, ambitions, and outcomes you are chasing?

These cracks in our lenses can pull us in many different directions. You might have a strong need for security or safety, be dealing with the same circumstances as James, or be dealing with something else entirely. I have seen many situations in which people identify as loners and deliberately limit their potential to avoid working with teams or forming close relationships.

It's impossible to list all the potential cracks in our lenses that can affect the driving forces in our lives, but the best way I have found to identify them is to connect with your daily actions and see how they align with your stated goals. When you see a shift in your actions that doesn't make sense in connection to your goals, engage "the inner two-year-old."

This has been an ongoing process in my life at every stage of growth and development. This process cannot be done just once. Rather, you must maintain this awareness and create checkpoints to conduct the needed reflection. This is how I connected to the issue from my past that I went over earlier in the book, where my brother's actions created a drive in me to pull back into the shadows. I had set goals and ambitious dreams, but I found myself pulling back from opportunities and failing to pursue them. Only by working through the process with "the inner two-year-old" was I able to uncover the "why" rooted in my childhood.

It is only natural to pull back in areas where you have deep programming or cracked lenses. The sources of these types of issues are all too frequently uncovered only *after* serious failures or broken dreams. If you don't do the hard work to uncover the root causes, this could be the catalyst for your failure.

I have worked with many clients who were drawn to remain in poverty despite the fact that they were working hard to find financial success, those who were destroying relationships that were the best thing for them, those turning away from the opportunities that could launch their careers, and those who were laced with self-inflicted wounds that diminished their potential outcome. The trauma, life circumstances, and programming from childhood create subconscious drivers that control the decisions or actions that we take unless we identify the source and confront the actions.

You will never regret taking the time and focus to connect back to where your cracks may stem from and identify how they are affecting your current situation. This awareness should be taken seriously, as the regrets from allowing these drivers to control your outcome will be heartbreaking.

Chasing the Ghost

Take a second and imagine this with me. You are a runner and have signed up for a race. You show up the day of the race, and they tell you there is no defined course or route, no specific distance, and no official finish line. Then they go on to tell you that if you don't win the race, you are a failure, not good enough, and a disappointment. There are no answers to your questions, just instructions to prepare yourself.

They rush you to the starting line, and at the sound of the horn, you take off running. You are pushing hard and keeping your head focused on one step at a time. But you cannot help thinking that you are off track, so you change directions multiple times, hoping that you are not going the wrong way. You are committed to finishing, but you don't know when your efforts will be enough. You want to see some signs of hope, like a support station, flags, or even other runners who might be better prepared than you, but nothing seems to be that beam of light.

This goes on until you feel utterly exhausted, hopeless, and like all your efforts are in vain. At some point, you give up and, in most cases, never run a race again. This is all because you felt like you were chasing a ghost finish line the entire time, and the expectations were never defined.

The crazy part is that most of us are chasing the ghosts in our lives, just like the scenario I set up above. This example shows the absurdity of the situation, but how many of us are burned out and exhausted because we have been given finish lines that don't exist? The most frustrating thing is that these kinds of situations reveal the cracks in our lenses, causing damage to how we view ourselves.

Hearing negative statements is painful. "You'll never be good enough." "You will never succeed." "You're going to fail." "You'll never amount to anything." "You're a loser." "You're a washout." "You're a failure." "What a dud." These kinds of statements may motivate people to work at disproving them, but the issue is that all of them lack definition. They ignite a drive that can lead to burnout, leaving people unfulfilled and failing to specify a definitive endpoint for disproving these statements.

The same is true in relationships, where a person from your childhood, a family member, or romantic partner has no clear expectations but always makes you feel like you are failing them. They want more effort, commitment, and action, but they never say what it takes to meet their relationship standards. When is good enough actually good enough? This is destructive not only to relationships but also to the individual on the receiving end.

I was in a relationship once where I allowed a person to lead me to believe I had all kinds of issues, and every issue in our relationship was blamed on me. This led me down a path of deep self-reflection and personal development. I was confronting issues from my past and driving deep into identifying areas where I could improve. As our relationship continued, the mud thrown in my direction seemed to be endless... and the relationship never got better.

I know you can see the writing on the wall, that I took the accusations seriously from this person who claimed to love me. You are correct: despite my efforts and improvements, the relationship remained unresolved. After all of that self-work, how calm the relationship was came down to how passive and patient I was, or, even worse, how selflessly I acted. I was dancing on eggshells, trying to keep the peace.

Looking back, this was massive manipulation, even sick, as this person used my desire to self-reflect and grow and become better as a tool to blame all the issues in our relationship on me. It became clear that even though I was imperfect, I was not the core of the relationship issues, and I spent a lot of time chasing ghosts.

The only benefit from this season is that I became very self-aware, learned a lot about myself, and became extremely willing to develop, grow, and become a better version of myself. However, the relationship created programming in me that left me scared and constantly feeling like I was not enough, and to be accepted and loved, I had to continually strive to be better.

In all honesty, this left many cracks in my lenses, distorting my view of myself, and furthered my insatiable need for growth and development.

Looking back at why I would have even started a dating relationship with someone like this, it makes sense that her personality was similar to aspects of my older brother, and I was drawn to the acceptance that initially came with the relationship, until she dropped the best-behavior act. A romantic relationship then reaffirmed the deep, fundamental wounds of my childhood, exacerbating the fractures and intensifying the pain. This type of programming can be damaging in the long run and potentially create drivers that keep us completely distracted from the vision and purpose of our lives.

In parenting relationships, many parents push their kids for greater output but don't take the time to properly celebrate their achievements. Or in some cases, they celebrate for the moment and then set a new level of expectation. The moving target is just as destructive to an individual's programming. It leads to a more checklist-style mentality rather than the ability to really enjoy successful achievements and outcomes, and each achievement has little to no emotional impact, only a bit of relief that something is taken off their list.

I have seen countless situations in which parents placed expectations on their children based on their own skill sets and abilities, without considering each child's individuality. The parents grew in frustration and pushed their children to higher levels of discipline and dedication, expecting greater results. The children conformed but never excelled at the expectations placed on them because it was not their greatest skill set or ability.

Such parents set a standard of acceptable behavior or outcomes that, for some children, is not even achievable. I have seen collegiate athletes who never turn professional and then push their kids so hard into sports that they completely burn them out with unrealistic expectations. I have encountered doctors and attorneys who impose their own expectations on their children, disregarding their children's desires, abilities, or greatest contributions.

If these people choose a different path or fail to meet expectations, they will live with a ghost-like finish line, knowing they didn't do what was expected. They won't stop pushing to be deemed acceptable or good enough to gain their parents' approval, but this is a moving target that they won't be able to hit.

Such scenarios are endless, and the damaged programming leaves so many people stuck chasing ghosts. Reflection is required. With James, until we uncovered the driving force from his past that created harmful cycles, he wasn't able to build true momentum toward his lighthouse. Acknowledging the ghosts we chase based on others' expectations and the damage from past relationships is the first major step toward controlling their effects on your life. It's important to reflect on where they stem from and then use a more mature lens to go back and reframe them, like we discussed in Chapter Five.

You must monitor these drivers by being aware of your actions. The days of chasing ghosts and destroying your forward momentum must end, and connecting back to the true driving forces that keep you moving down that pathway should become a daily habit.

Fuel Requires Depth

In working with countless entrepreneurs and high achievers, I have heard just about every fuel source people use to stay inspired. People often connect with their most immediate motivators, but they miss the deeper, true drivers in their lives. The most common situation is when people become "sprinters." They get excited and start moving too fast toward their goal but then burn out quickly after encountering hardships and resistance.

This is why, when I discuss the fuel that fills your tank for the journey, it needs to have depth—the type of fuel that will not burn out upon hitting resistance. I am not saying that you cannot use the surface-level fuel to get you moving, but you have to have the deeper fuel to maintain the type of effort needed. I have found that the deeper I go, the more powerful the fuel becomes, lasting well beyond the hardships or difficulties I face on the journey.

I tend to think about fuel in a similar way to a campfire: the REI Co-op breaks down the three required fuel sources as tinder, kindling, and firewood, stating, *"Tinder includes small twigs, dry leaves, needles, or forest duff; kindling consists of small sticks, typically less than one inch around, and firewood is any larger piece of wood and is what will keep your fire going long into the night."*

When you look at your life, you can identify layers of fuel, such as the tinder. You can visualize tinder in ways like proving people wrong, competing with others, or setting short-term goals for yourself. The kindling goes deeper, like serving the needs of others, providing security, or even pursuing longer-term goals for your life.

The firewood is what you are really looking for, and this is what comes together to create the heart of the fire. It becomes the central fuel source that keeps the fire burning hot for a long time. For you, this might mean making a difference in others' lives, supporting others to reach a better life, being a good example for your children, or changing what some would consider generational curses in your family line.

Understanding these different fuel sources and connecting them to your life is of extreme importance. Most people I encounter understand the motivational and driving forces in their lives, but they struggle to connect with the depth needed to reach what I call their "heart fuel."

Heart fuel is a tough concept for many of us to grasp. Often, this involves looking at aspects of our lives we have "boxed up and put in the basement," those things we find ourselves resistant to going back and revisiting. I know that revisiting the past and confronting trauma and difficulties can be painful, but approaching it with the right mindset can uncover fuel sources and bring purpose.

One of the most difficult moments in my life, which I discussed earlier in this book, was the darkness that I found myself in and whether I wanted to continue on. There were days when I felt it would be easier to just be done rather than keep pushing forward. Now, I leverage that dark time as one of the greatest sources of heart fuel, as I know how dark things can get. I understand that hope feels swallowed by the shadows cast by the hardships you face. The hardships I have faced drive me to dedicate my life to helping others.

Understand that it doesn't matter what you have done, what has happened to you, or what you are in the midst of dealing with; what matters is how you show up today. The future that is in front of you is based on what you make of it. Connecting to the core of who you are and what you are built to take on allows you to chase your future and create new dreams you could never have imagined were yours.

I felt alone during those hard times, but I am grateful to God that He showed up and told me that the journey I was on wasn't only for me. I had to push through and create greatness on the other side, with His help, guidance, and support, to give others hope. Returning to my basement, where these difficult moments and seasons reside, is not an easy task for me. Yet to have the greatest possible impact, I know I have to return to those moments with the right frame, leverage the fuel they provide, and connect to the principles I can use to support others.

Each of us has difficulties and even relationships from our past that have created hurt, hardships, and even trauma. I need you to think deeply about those and find every possible source of fuel that can be generated from them and put into your tank to keep you motivated toward your dreams. Just like with a campfire, you will need fuel sources of all types to ensure you "catch fire" and have the ability to continue the burn to generate the heat needed.

The life you are called to live isn't just about making money or achieving some goals you set that bring attention to how awesome you are. The life you have been built to take on goes way beyond the surface, and those who fully connect to their purpose can tap into a fuel source like no other. Yes, certain hurts and situations can create those cracked lenses and derail our actions, but if we learn to channel our focus to the core aspects of supporting others through their darkness, it can be extremely powerful. The circumstances of our pasts can never be changed, but with God's help, we can redeem what was intended to harm us and leverage it to create change and healing for others.

I am extremely passionate about this topic, and when I have the opportunity to speak to groups, I find that the more open I am about the hardships and crazy life situations I have encountered, the greater the impact I have. The deeper I allow my emotions to go and the more I am open about the rough reality I have experienced, the more those who are listening have the ability to connect to their own fuel. This is not easy, especially for people like me, who were trained as police officers to internalize rather than process emotions. The fuel inside me for having the impact I am capable of is greater than the fuel inside me for comfort and security when dealing with past situations.

The depth of fuel that you lock into isn't simple, easy, or a one-time event; it is rather an ongoing leveraging of the heart of the fire that you create by uncovering the logs that need to be placed in. This fuel, along with all the other driving forces connected to your "lighthouse," needs to be identified, detailed, and laid out, ready to be part of the ongoing inspiration that pushes you harder than you have ever been. You must lock in the fuel needed to accomplish all that you have been entrusted with.

Oxygen Required

Once your fire is ignited, it's important to keep the oxygen flowing so it can continue to burn. We all need oxygen, or the fire will die out. To some, "oxygen" is having a steady flow of reminders back to the deep-rooted fuel that drives motivation. This might be a daily reflection on the core aspects included in your heart fuel and the why behind each one. Others might be able to use a statement about people they are pushing to impact. Some even have a token or small object that helps them connect immediately to their deep drivers.

It is important to identify the ways you keep that oxygen flowing and the fuel driving that fire. It is easy, amid the busyness of life, to allow these deep-rooted fuel sources to slide back into the shadows of our basement. When this happens, we lose sight of the purpose of surfacing those situations or experiences. You might default to storing them and forgetting them to eliminate associated pain.

You must always look at those situations with the right frame and acknowledge the purpose they serve, rather than soaking in the pain and hurt of the past. The most important aspect here is to keep your focus on your why. Staying locked in to your fuel system and connecting to it frequently allows the fire to burn bright and the fuel to ignite change.

Many people have a need to acknowledge positive movements and incremental gains. It is important to take the time to celebrate the milestones, allowing yourself to connect back to the starting point and the desired end point, and to identify the growth. You might have your own way of seeing this or of understanding your need for this type of inspiration on the journey.

You have to be honest with yourself to determine whether something is oxygen to your fire and whether it will be a motivator to keep you going. I find it increasingly important to take time to pause and celebrate the gains as I continue on my impact journey. For some, this should be daily, and for others, there should be an ongoing process of allowing yourself to live in the moments when you strive and hit achievements.

You shouldn't live your life in checklist mode. The celebration of journey wins can provide immense encouragement. You cannot let your fuel burn out by only seeing the end result as a point to celebrate.

To be honest, I have struggled with allowing celebration in my life. My biggest successes would feel no greater than the relief of checking them off my list. I am getting better at acknowledging my wins and getting excited about crossing the finish line on projects or goals, but I am still working on the emotional side of celebrating and having feelings beyond only the relief of completing a goal.

This message is for you and for me: we need to take the time to see our gains, small wins, and incremental growth, creating milestones and celebrating those moments when we gain ground.

There isn't any specific requirement for maintaining the flow of oxygen into your fire and fuel system. This is a reflective process that you should walk through. The core focus is that your fueled fire requires oxygen to continue burning brightly and creating life-changing outcomes. You must lock in the processes, actions, and acknowledgments that feed your fuel-filled fire.

Identify the Extinguishers

As you consider the aspects that feed your fire, it is important to identify the extinguishers, those things that choke out your flame and destroy your fuel pack. You must reflect on what kills your momentum. This is very different for each person, and a part of each of our pasts will influence how we respond to the diverse experiences in our lives.

As I discussed, sometimes I have trouble seeing my achievements as nothing more than a completed checklist item. Celebrating them hasn't always been a strength of mine, and even just telling others about my wins has been difficult. This goes back to my fundamental issues with the cracked lenses and my struggle with the celebration.

Growing up, my siblings reacted poorly to my celebrations, making me reluctant to celebrate my successes to avoid their negative feelings. The extinguisher in this situation from my past is the fear of others' reactions to my success.

This, along with other cracked lenses I have shared about my life, such as my unquenchable thirst for growth due to my relationships and never feeling good enough, meant that the checklist I created was merely a ladder toward seeking love or acceptance. The moving target and ghost finish lines were the extinguishers for my spirit. I felt as though no matter what I accomplished, new things were always added to the list of how I was a failure or never good enough.

Reflection often requires identifying those extinguishers, which may include aspects of holdbacks, delays, and even relational turmoil. I have worked with many people whose fuel seemed to be completely lost when they were having issues in their marriage or trouble with their kids. I understand that life has many difficulties and that relationships are tough to manage, but this should not completely choke out your fire.

I strongly encourage you to look deeper into why these distractions, roadblocks, and difficulties extinguish your growth or progress. This demonstrates the value of a deep-rooted fuel system. Certain things may be able to cause disturbance to your flame, but they should not be able to choke out the flame because of the fuel system you have locked in.

Furthermore, some aspects are extremely difficult to confront, and raw honesty is needed. When you face the truth of who you are, the tides in your life, and the deep-rooted fuel you need to lock into, you often realize that you haven't been living up to your potential. This might be in how you have handled yourself with your family, your relationships, your business, your finances, your walk with God, or your physical well-being.

The extinguisher is the pride that keeps you from confronting your past failures and having hard conversations with those affected when you show up as a lesser version of who you are called to be. What are the conversations that you need to have with those loved ones so that you can take ownership of your past actions? Are there people to whom you need to own up for the hurt you caused? What secrets are gnawing at your soul, keeping you from taking the actions that can be life-changing for you, your family, and your future?

Failing to have these conversations leads to feelings of unworthiness, which hold you back from becoming the person you are called to be. Get it all out in the open, handle the criticism and failure, and be held accountable for the ways you have handled yourself. This isn't easy, but you must face "hard";

it can either contribute to your growth and development or extinguish your fire and deplete your fuel.

The dynamics of relationships, expectations, and navigating the past to break free and chase your future can feel like a dance. I will tell you directly that there are some people in your life who will not understand the direction you are choosing to go, and some who might even mock you or tell you that you are crazy. I have encountered a significant number of individuals in my life with whom I had to establish strict boundaries in our relationship as they began to drain my energy.

Take the time to reflect on and identify who in your life could be holding you back from taking the actions required to become the greatest version of yourself. Who could be impeding your ability to fully embrace your strengths and relentlessly pursue your "lighthouse"? You cannot allow what others might think of your growth to extinguish your fire.

I am not talking about you considering a divorce or breaking up your families, as there can be great healing when you take complete ownership of your failures and show a consistent pattern of growth and forward development. While pressing the "eject" button may seem like a simple solution, it may not be the best one. You must work hard to be the best spouse and parent and pursue your other goals.

The extinguishers in your life can have a drastic effect on the momentum you build. The system you leverage to fuel your fire must be deeply rooted and have a greater purpose than anything surface-level. The combination of you connecting to the displayed version of who you are capable of becoming, the lighthouse that is your guide, and the fuel system to keep you driven and motivated, becomes the death of complacency and the end of any excuses you have allowed yourself to live in.

Paint the picture of what you can chase after and the impact you can have in your life once you truly believe in what is possible with this new reality. The fuel you choose to fill your tank with can help you thrive through any circumstance and overcome any barriers you encounter. Connecting to the deep fuel that can be at the heart of your fire brings true drive and ambition, while acknowledging drivers through our cracked lenses creates awareness of potential derailers. The full perspective and understanding of both of these are required in each of our lives to keep us driving toward our lighthouse with focused dedication.

CHAPTER 9

Focus Over Feelings

Have you ever been asked a question that stopped you in your tracks? Was the question so challenging that it compelled you to engage in a challenging conversation with yourself? I recently appeared on a podcast, and the format was that the current guest must answer a question left behind by the guest from the previous episode. The host laid out the question I had to answer: "What do you want to be engraved on your tombstone?"

I thought for just a moment, then responded with something heartfelt, like, "He left it all here. He gave this his all." At that moment, it felt so easy to come up with this statement, but it would be the start of a tug at my heart. Realizing what it meant gave me pause. Integrating that truth into my personal lighthouse wasn't easy; it left me stumbling over my next steps for a short while.

The days of reflection that followed left me with moments of regret, sadness, and even frustration over time wasted. I thought through the "I love yous" that had not been said, the friendships that had been lost, the mistakes that had derailed my progress, and the distractions that had pulled my attention off track.

Then, as I dug deep into this statement about how I want my life defined, there was a moment of clarity.

I am not dead yet, and the definition of my life has not yet been etched into stone. I still have time, and my story is not over. I get to make the choice as to how I am going to show up every day moving forward, not letting the past dictate, distract, or derail the way I deploy into each day. I have a decision to make: am I going to allow the past to be the deciding factor, or am I going to control the way I advance and pursue the opportunities in front of me?

As I worked through all of this, I was reminded of when I was hired as a police officer. I was nineteen years old, and I'll gladly admit I didn't have the life experience to prepare me for some of the situations I would face. Some would even say I was a little sheltered as a kid and didn't know the extent of how bad the streets could be, especially as a police officer. I had an excitement for helping people and saw more of the optimistic side of what the career could look like as I began my training.

One of my training officers, Officer Ertel, took it upon himself to make sure that I was prepared not just to gain the knowledge to get through training, but more importantly, to survive the streets. He persistently instilled in me the belief that darkness always lurks, emphasizing the importance of being prepared and trained for every moment. He routinely stated this was a requirement to survive as a cop.

He laid out a simple principle that left me forever impacted: release what happened on the last emergency call, the last shift, and even your personal life; focus on how to survive and overcome the darkness in each present situation you are in; and take each emergency and non-emergency call with the utmost seriousness, knowing that there are many people out there waiting for you to get their opportunity to harm you.

It is very easy to get distracted, focusing on how you could have handled prior situations better, and even starting to doubt yourself. You cannot change the past; what matters is the situation you are facing right now. Trust your preparation, training, and planning, then take action to the greatest of your ability. After a tough situation, take a moment to think about how you could have been better prepared or acted, then move on. You cannot allow distractions to get you off focus. You have to lock in for the moment that is in front of you. What defines you is not what you have done in the past, but rather the situation you are facing.

Officer Ertel's passion and words have resonated with me not only during my days in law enforcement but also as an entrepreneur, father, husband, and leader. I am not talking about the darkness coming after me in the form of dirty diapers, honey-do lists, and other demands for my attention. I am talking about the ability to release and remain in focus. This is a very difficult thing for most high achievers, driven individuals, and those who are on their path to greatness.

It is easy for you and me to live in the realm of "what ifs" and do-overs. I know in my head, I say often, *I should have seen that coming,* or, *If I had only known this back then,* and even moments of *Man, that really sucks; I should have known.* We then replay all the aspects we should have identified, known, or forecasted and live in a world where there's a redo button.

The issue is that, with these tendencies, a flood of emotions starts to take over. We become frustrated with ourselves, get hard on ourselves, and even verbally belittle ourselves. Then comes regret, feelings of failure, and so many other emotions that can drive us down some dark paths. I have been there and have felt some hopeless moments at the hand of my own self-inflicted wounds, coupled with the 20/20 vision that comes with hindsight.

There are times when you may feel as though you blew your one big opportunity or feel as if you will never be able to have your chance to make things right. Officer Ertel warned me that you can't move forward while looking back, even though there are many ways to view the past. Yes, learn from the lessons, identify the missteps, and plan for additional training, but don't let it distract you from the present.

Being reminded of all of this helped me lock back into the moment and reconnect to my core principles, steering course toward my lighthouse every day. Now, as I look at the notes and details I've made about my lighthouse I'm aiming toward, I have written at the top, *"He left it all here; he gave this his all."* This keeps me focused on relentlessly pushing for the impact I am chasing after and the lives I am striving to be a light for.

There are days when my feelings conflict with my life's dedication, and those feelings are not always supportive; however, my locked-in focus becomes the guiding principle for how I will show up. I stay connected to the hope that I am not done yet, and in my heart, I'm locked into the fact that I am just getting started. The truth I had to cling to is the same one I am pushing you to focus on: you are not defined by what was but by what is and will be. It's all about this moment, this day, and how you show up from now on.

Your actions have power. They create new history and, most importantly, new definitions. The ability to push forward and chase a better life, a greater future, and a clearer sense of who you are and what you can do always starts with this moment and how you handle today.

The Intersection

The truth I have to admit to you is that I have been laying out an infrastructure to lead up to this moment to tie in the importance of focus. I have concocted an evil plan to help you understand how to be more focused without you even knowing it. Well, I know it isn't quite evil, but it's definitely intentional.

I have laid out some core principles throughout this book that all come together to provide you with clarity and a vision of what your life should look like. To complete this, you need to connect to the "displayed version" of who you are built to become, lock into the "fuel" that keeps you motivated, and keep your eyes set on the "lighthouse" for your forever goals and ambitions. I have also encouraged you to recognize the "tides" and influences that pull you in different directions.

Each element is pertinent, but they all intersect at the point that provides a clear direction for your focused action. If any one of these elements is missing, the clarity is skewed and could misdirect you. This is why I have laid the foundation throughout the book: to help you gain complete clarity on the direction you need to push all your actions toward.

Focus is one of the most important aspects of each of our lives, and when coupled with action, it becomes a dynamic force that builds momentum. This intersection is the needle of your compass, always giving you a clear direction. I want to challenge you to work back through each vital element to ensure that you have done the work to gain the accurate guidepost to measure every opportunity and action against. You might have done some of the work and even locked in on certain aspects, but good luck racing forward when your vehicle is missing a wheel. This is how you find yourself running in circles.

The core pillars that I have covered are not just here for your amusement or for you to read more of my life stories; rather, they are fundamentally required for you to achieve the greatest results that you are capable of. Your steps and actions will yield dynamic results only after you take the time to fully develop each of these in your life and address how your cracked lenses can be a derailing factor.

I want you to know that I'm not saying this as someone who has done everything right over the last twenty years but as someone who has made a lot of mistakes. I had to figure out where I went wrong and what I missed on multiple occasions. I dedicated myself to navigating the landmines and self-imposed obstacles to gain an understanding of my life as well as to assist others on their journeys. I didn't have anyone to turn to for help or the ability to locate and hire someone to fast-track me around the failure points, so I promised myself I would become that for others.

I cannot stress enough to you the importance of having these core principles locked in place and having a full understanding of who you are and what you are capable of. The dreams you are laying out for the rest of your life require you to have full focus and relentless drive. Putting in the effort to understand how these principles work together creates a pull on the needle of your compass to guide your way. The *amount* of action is not what creates momentum toward your lighthouse; it is your continuous, focused action.

Feelings Are Fleeting

Do you ever get on those kicks, wanting to become a physical machine by going hard and slaying every opportunity to "get some gains in"? Or maybe you get excited about a new tool and start building all kinds of stuff, knocking out your honey-do list. For others, it is the excitement of a new business venture and the hyperfocus you can lock in. Do you get inspired at events and hit the ground running when you get home?

Be honest: how long can you keep up the same pace or dedication after the initial excitement? This is a huge issue for far too many people: they get excited, motivated, or even inspired to take new action, but the foundation behind it is usually tied to someone else's story, experience, or outcomes. The feelings fade, and the actions subside. The foundation of the entire movement was surface-level and based on feelings.

Getting hit in the face with the reality of the multitude of work that is required to make real changes and create new life habits can bring an entirely different feeling that overrides and engulfs the original feeling and excitement. Next, burnout may set in, and after that, the lure of the next big feeling wave looms before you. This won't just happen to you; a lot of people struggle with chasing the next shiny object that can provide a dopamine hit and rush of excitement.

All too many motivational speakers prey on people's excitement... and then offer to provide a life-changing experience that will cost them only $5,000. I don't want to bash all speakers, but I have come across many who focus more on profit by influencing people's feelings rather than helping them make real changes.

I understand that people need more than just a one-hour keynote to make real changes in their lives. When I get on stage, I give it my all to help people make serious moves. Then I will offer a free next step to keep their learning moving forward. I do not believe in just inspiring or motivating people; I am dedicated to helping people move past those initial feelings and into real-life change. American entrepreneur, author, and motivational speaker Jim Rohn has one of my favorite quotes of all time, and I take this seriously: *"Motivation alone is not enough. If you have an idiot and you motivate him, now you have a motivated idiot."*

I am not saying that anyone I speak in front of is an idiot; rather, I see this as an opportunity to unlock a new area in someone's life or open their eyes to a new understanding, which requires additional guidance. That is why I provide follow-up support through a free program after a speaking engagement. I never want someone to feel motivated and then not have next steps available for them.

You will have days when you don't want to push yourself and do uncomfortable things. Feelings are based on circumstances and situations; often, they are triggered by our past experiences rather than by facts, the future, or potential. This is where you have to connect to your focus, detail out your plan, set your lighthouse, and push toward that direction, no matter what feelings may come up. Your actions must be guided by principles and standards for how you will show up each day. These should all be based on what is required of you in order to be able to reach that lighthouse.

Ben Newman, USA Today Top 5 Coach in the World, TOP 50 Keynote Speaker, and 2x Wall Street Journal Best Seller, has a saying when it comes to what it takes to reach greatness and what it requires from you: *"Long obedience in the same direction with aggressive patience."* I don't know the last time you have been in a season that required aggressive patience or any patience at all, but for me, they are extremely difficult on my feelings. Many times, I want to chase another shiny object or have conflicting feelings about giving up or changing directions. This is why our feelings cannot be our drivers or keep us on track; we have to push deeper and go past the feelings that come and go.

The shifting of feelings can seem like the changing of tides: one day, you are on fire, pushing hard at the process, and the next, you want the eject button. I get that completely, and those shifting feelings will happen more times than you can count, which is why your foundation needs to be set and your choice already made to go hard, build momentum, and focus your actions.

"This Play"

In my son's football league, there are multiple locations with different teams and league rankings. One season, the director of the league asked me to coach a team at a different location, and, trying to support the league, I said yes. I didn't know I was getting all the unpaired, extra kids, some new to the league.

The practices were quite interesting. Trying to prepare for the first game, I had some of the kids who had never caught a football before. It was a challenging start to the season. I would love to report that in the first game, we came out and held our own, but the reality is that we were destroyed. We had to be put under the mercy rule, which let us start on the 40-yard line and prevented the other team from rushing the quarterback.

It was a tough blow to the team, my son, and my pride as the coach. I had to go back to the drawing board on how I was going to handle this team because, in all the prior seasons, the majority of my players had been repeat players and all dialed in. In my reflection, I connected back to major points in the game where the players lost heart and were not putting forth full effort. I had to connect to how I handled those moments. Yes, I offered encouragement, but I didn't take the time to help them recenter.

Moving into the next practice, I walked the team through what I called the "this play" mentality. I told them about the story of Officer Ertel and explained to them that all that mattered was how they showed up in this moment and in this play. I walked them through strategies for resetting after a bad play, a tough call, and even a big mistake. We explored how to recenter ourselves and be fully present in each play.

Entering the second game with a change of perspective on how to manage this group, which I felt was like a bunch of wild stallions, we were able to lock into a groove. The team successfully reset, recentered, and maintained focus throughout every play. There were interceptions, balls dropped, and failed defensive plays, but the team stayed focused. This was a game we played against the number one team in the league, and the end result was not what we wanted. But how we showed up allowed us to leave the game with our heads held high.

Over the next few weeks of hard work and practice, maintaining the core focus of the "this play" mentality, the team came together and started winning. After a few wins, we started dominating, and the team's morale reached heights I'd thought were impossible with this squirrely group. The team was locked in and would reset and refocus for every play, never allowing what had just occurred to rock their foundation.

To this day, this was my favorite team I have ever coached. They weren't the greatest players, and they definitely weren't the group that I would have selected, but they became dedicated and had the greatest growth. We ended the season as the number two team. We defeated the number one team in the regular season, but in the championship game, we lost by one touchdown. Our team felt as though we had already won by going from the last team in the league to playing in the championship.

I share this story with you because I feel it is important to connect you to the same mentality of "this play." I know there are tough days, brutal beatings, and even failures that haunt you, but you have to connect to a process that gets your focus locked in, where you recenter and get ready to charge forward.

My morning routine is set up so I focus on my learning, development, and relationship with God. This one-hour process helps me recenter and be ready for what the day may bring. The ability to control my emotions and feelings to maximize my momentum is a vital skill. This does require me, at times, to identify my feelings, engaging my "inner two-year-old" to help determine why and where some of the feelings come from. This allows me to identify which items I need to release and what is within my control or ability to create a better outcome. This also helps me focus on which action items need to be prioritized based on their alignment with my lighthouse.

Our wide-ranging feelings often do not drive us to take the greatest actions needed to reach our lighthouse. This is why we have to engage in our own process of resetting and refocusing on "this play" in front of us. You have to create a process for releasing what has happened in the past and letting go of mistakes, failures, and feelings from yesterday so you can connect back to this moment in front of you.

Define the Sidelines

You can now see that defining the field of play is necessary, based on the roadmap and journey we've taken. There are many approaches to pursuing different outcomes aggressively in our lives. Each of us needs to be honest with ourselves and reflective about our habits and behaviors. Doing this allows us to identify whether we are taking actions that properly move us down the field and which aspects might be out of bounds.

Also, for some, this might require you to define what it looks like to be sitting on the sidelines. I understand firsthand how difficult some actions might be and what it takes to overcome fears, insecurities, and other areas holding you back. The sidelines can be a draw for you and seem safe and secure, but what I want you to understand is that by sitting on the sidelines, you are guaranteeing your failure. At least when you are on the field and taking daily actions, you have an opportunity to advance down the field and move toward your goal line.

This is why you need a clear definition of what it means to live on the sidelines. You also need to define the field of play and the actions you are taking that are clearly within it and begin moving in the appropriate direction. The issue is that people often take action but lack the definition, which can allow for a lot of effort to be wasted with unfocused movements. The more parameters we can set in our lives, the faster we can recognize when we go out of bounds.

This is also a great reason why it is important to have accountability, as well as someone in your corner who guides you regularly. Some of my clients bring a wealth of great ideas, and part of my role in their lives involves assisting them in aligning these ideas with their core values and the development of their personal goals. This leads to some quite entertaining conversations but also provides a safe place to work through the options. In the end, it saves a lot of wasted time, effort, and frustration.

A third party can help you if you know your field's definition and what it means to be on the sidelines. You must either develop these definitions yourself or involve others; you cannot develop all of them extrinsically. You have to own the boundaries you will be required to adhere to. The boundaries, lines of delineation, and definition of riding the bench are all important for you to create to ensure you are staying in bounds and actually driving down your field of play.

The Actions That Bring Life

As you reflect and connect to the parameters that are keeping you in the game, it is important to focus even deeper on what actions are required of you to bring your dreams to life. This is not just about achieving some goals or accomplishing what others have said couldn't be done. This is about your dreams and what you are capable of chasing after and accomplishing.

I encouraged you earlier in this book to challenge everything, including what your dreams are made of. I will be honest: it is the third type of dream that still challenges me almost every week: *What are the dreams that I still don't know can be mine?* Every time I feel I have pushed my goals and ambitions to the extreme, a new level of awareness always shines through. As my focused actions continually point in the right direction, moving me toward my lighthouse, a new level of life emerges, and greater dreams are uncovered.

This can be the same for you. What dreams do you not know could be yours? Only when you are faithful with your focus and action steps, moving toward the greatest version of yourself and continually chasing your lighthouse, do new levels of capability become opportunities for you. Think about it as the new growth of a plant: each phase brings about bright and beautiful colors and potential new heights for the plant. Think of it like the new growth of a plant: while each phase brings vibrant color and exciting new heights, the real power lies in what happens next. As that expansion stabilizes, it hardens into a foundation of structural integrity, a 'solid ground' that is strong enough to support the next surge of progress. This compounding cycle of reaching and then reinforcing is what allows the transformation of today's ceiling into tomorrow's floor, ultimately pushing the potential far beyond what was previously possible.

The compound effect of being disciplined to take focused action and consistently move toward your lighthouse provides an entirely new vision for your greatest capabilities. This is why I feel it is important to reflect on what actions you are taking that bring new growth. What are the areas of your life that, when you take focused action toward building momentum, allow for an expansion of what you knew was possible? What are the action steps you take that encourage you to chase harder toward your lighthouse? What are those areas of discomfort that, when you push through, can become a new foundation to build on?

List out the top actions, habits, and utilizations of your skill sets and abilities that create the greatest momentum toward your dreams. Take inventory of the actions that will build progress toward becoming the displayed version of yourself. Also, connect and identify the most progressive actions that drive you furthest down the road toward your lighthouse.

Working through these questions and detailing the actions that are aligned with the outcomes you are striving toward is not just for the days you are motivated and progressing. They are even more important on days when your feelings seem to get in the way, and your motivation is lacking. Those days are critical for keeping the actions in play and moving forward.

Taking action when you don't feel like it is a great reflection of your discipline and, even more importantly, a reflection of how it affects your body. There has been a lot of research on the anterior mid-cingulate cortex (aMCC) in our brains and on the structural changes that occur when we take actions we are resistant to. The research goes deep into the aspects of the aMCC's connection to tenacity, motivation, and willpower, all factors that can affect people on their success journey.

The Neuroscience School, led by Dr. Irena O'Brien, breaks it down in a very simple way: *"Engaging in challenging tasks can strengthen the aMCC. Like working out a muscle, these challenges can help increase the aMCC's capacity, enhancing our overall willpower in any domain."* Challenges are like a muscle that builds the more you take action when you are resistant. The opposite is also true when you give in to the temptation to let resistance win; when this happens, it becomes more difficult the next time you want to take action.

There is a need, and some would even say a requirement, to set goals and create ambitious dreams for your life and then to consistently take actions that require us to be challenged. By engaging in these, we are continuing our growth but also enhancing our ability to take on even greater challenges. This all brings an entirely different vantage point to the concept of actions that bring life, as it emphasizes the importance of embracing challenges as essential components of personal growth and fulfillment.

The question to ask yourself at this point is: how are your actions aligning with your greatest goals? If you sat down for a serious conversation with yourself, would you say you're moving with the momentum needed to claim the dreams you once thought were out of reach? Are you actually doing the work, or are you just talking about your dreams? How are you moving each day to challenge yourself and get uncomfortable in your progress?

The important aspects here are not just being able to see and connect to dreams you never thought possible for you, but, most importantly, taking daily actions that move you forward on the path to make them your reality. Each day, you should be challenging yourself to increase your progress beyond your comfort zone, which, in turn, will increase your aMCC's capacity for greater action. This is all to ensure your growth and development and to help you achieve results that move you toward your greatest future.

Your actions are either bringing life to the future that you are capable of achieving or bringing death to the dreams that you have or once had. There is no middle ground of staying in one spot, like you are somehow not succeeding and also not failing. You are either driving toward your goals and chasing your dreams, or you are allowing them to slip away and break. If you say yes to the actions required to move toward your dreams, you are saying no to complacency, easy roads, and even to your fears and insecurities.

You have to be very careful about what you say yes to and what you say no to, because there is always another side. If you say yes to catering to your feelings and allowing them to drive your decisions, you are also saying no to the momentum you should be building that day. If you say yes to comfort and give in to your fears, you are saying no to overcoming and conquering the next step toward your greatness.

I understand completely what you are feeling right now; it is not easy to live in a world of constant growth and development. Future rewards require self-sacrifice, days of denying yourself comfort and security, and never catering to many of your feelings. I have looked at my wife many times and told her that I wish, for just a day, to know what it feels like not to have the intense, intrinsic drive to better myself. But I'm very glad that life has made me this way, even if it's hard to live in my skin some days. Constantly pushing myself, developing, and improving brings life to my spirit. I know I am a work in progress, and I still struggle in many ways, but knowing I still have much to achieve keeps me moving forward in every area of my life.

You have to come to terms with these same situations and aspects of who you are, as well as what growth and development are required for you to constantly gain ground. Your ability to lock into growth that can only come from the discipline of consistently taking focused action will be what brings life to your dreams.

Focus Factor

Many people are searching for a quick, easy way to get rich or a single-source solution for achieving a better life. They end up chasing so many shiny objects with claimed results that others package them and sell them. They spend countless hours and dollars trying to find the shortcuts and painless steps needed to get results. Unfortunately, these sidetracks and money pits often lead to frustration and burnout.

Yes, it would have been incredible to find my success and financial freedom by just throwing $995 at some influencer. I could have received a special program that would have removed all the hardships and made me wealthy in 180 days rather than sixteen years of the grind, but that isn't how success works. Your dreams won't come true this way, and the required journey is the only way to uncover the best version of yourself.

Part of the reason the gains are so sweet is that you are willing to put in the hard work and effort required. It is only natural to want to skip all the pain, hardship, and suffering that it might take for you to be able to reach your lighthouse, but a part of setting these types of goals for your life is that you have to become the person who is capable of achieving those great things. I am all about getting the right consultant or coach to help navigate the storms and create faster momentum when efforts are focused and channeled, but there are no magical systems that can remove the requirement for dedicated actions.

If you want the fast track, I will lay it out here for you. The more focused you are on your journey, the greater the outcomes you will create for your life. I guarantee that if you do not focus, your life will reflect failure in your output. Focus is the ingredient that, at times, seems like the secret that no one can lock into. Look around at the people around you who claim to be "hungry" and "driven," moving forward on their success journey. Identify the ones who appear to be locked in and focused and then those who are lacking focus. Pay attention to the difference in momentum and who achieves greater results.

I work with many individuals, and while none of them lack drive and ambition, the prior outcomes in their lives scream a lack of focus. Getting them dialed in with the right ability to channel that drive and ambition in a focused direction becomes the game-changer and catalyst for their journey. There are many ways for people to become successful, but you have to connect the pieces to the intersection that I explained earlier in this chapter. From there, you should be able to create focus. You can't continue to let feelings derail your progress and shiny objects distract your actions.

This book is all about your ability to dream of goals, ambitions, and legacy. Even more importantly, I have laid out this entire book in a way that the dreams you cast for your life should become your reality. Removing the cracks in your lenses while building the right, focused actions creates a dynamic combination of development and growth.

Yes, it will take hard work and extreme effort on your part, but now you can pursue your future with more confidence because you've locked into these core principles. The exciting part is that your life is at your fingertips, and you get to write your future. Focus becomes the difference between those who just want and those who achieve. There are no second chances for this life, and you can create all the goals, ambitions, and outcomes you want, but if you are not taking focused action, you will face regret. This becomes the choice that you get to make: continue being derailed by emotions, feelings, and distractions, or lock in to the focus that guides your actions.

CHAPTER 10

Your Legacy Is Waiting

As she lay in the hospital bed, connected to all the machines keeping her alive, the doctors expressed that there was nothing more that they could do. They had given her all the antibiotics possible and completed an exploratory surgery but found nothing that could have been the cause. They explained they had followed all available protocols, but the moments at hand were all that they could guarantee.

After days of working through every possibility of where this freak occurrence had come from, there were still no clear explanations. They expressed that the likelihood of her pulling through was in the single-digit percentages. What started as symptoms similar to a stomach bug or food poisoning turned out to be the onset of what became toxic shock. Her body was fighting to survive by pooling all her blood to her main body mass, and her limbs began turning black from the lack of blood supply. There were no answers and no clear affected areas to treat from which the infection could have stemmed.

To add to the pressure, the doctors had to explain that because of the "do not resuscitate" request they had on file, they could only keep her on life support for two more days. The rules they had to follow were strict, and they had only been able to keep her alive this long because of the surgery and the rules connected to recovery. The time was coming to a close that allowed them to utilize life support, and they had no more options.

This woman, lying in a hospital bed, had lived her life in a way that made her a light in the darkness to all who knew her. She'd dedicated her life to impacting lives and serving others in sacrificial ways that demonstrated nothing but love. As a mother, she'd demonstrated the right balance of boundaries, guidance, love, and support. All of her children would praise her for the patience and love she demonstrated as she juggled the four of them with their hyperactive, passionate, and headstrong natures.

After raising her own children, volunteering at church, and assisting ministries with developing their curriculum and programs, all out of the kindness of her heart, she felt called to make an even bigger impact. She returned to formal education to get her bachelor's and master's degrees so she could become a licensed mental health counselor with a focus on those who were dealing with trauma and extreme hardship. Her heart was for the hurting, lost, and troubled. She was dedicated to bringing them hope, not only to help them through their recovery but also to guide them to a greater future. The life she lived up to this point was self-sacrificing, supportive, loving, and full of joy.

Watching as her life appeared to be drained from her body, her husband was in complete disbelief and crushed in his spirit, but he knew that if it was God's will, she would pull through. At this point, when doctors had given up hope, he knew there was only one option: he locked in on a passage in the Bible, James 5:14–15a. In the New International Version (NIV), it states, *"Is anyone among you sick? Let them call the elders of the church to pray over them and anoint them with oil in the name of the Lord. And the prayer offered in faith will make the sick person well; the Lord will raise them up."*

This was exactly what he did. He called the pastor of his church, and the next morning, the pastor came and prayed over his wife and anointed her with oil. The prayers were lifted up in that exact moment and continued by the family, the church family, and the church elders.

What happened in the next twenty-four hours was nothing short of a miracle. Even the doctors were left baffled with no medical explanation. She went from a declining state, with the inevitable only being delayed, all the way to being fully conscious and able to talk. She was removed from all support except the dialysis machine. This last machine was only required for an additional twenty-four hours.

This was an incredible intervention that could only be credited to God, and in all the joy, there also came the acknowledgment of the tough journey ahead. Even though God had stepped in and saved her from death, there were still effects from the toxic shock on her body. The pulling of blood to her main body mass had left her extremities with permanent damage.

The days that followed involved countless trips to the hyperbaric chamber, painstaking treatments of the affected areas, and the doom of amputations. She held tightly to the promises of God and deepened her relationship with Jesus Christ. This treacherous period was the brightening of her light and her impact on people who knew her. Watching the way she walked through these days, dealt with unimaginable pain while caring for others, and lived in faith that God had a plan was more than enough to deepen others' faith.

While she was in the hospital and recovery facilities, she dedicated herself to sharing the love of Jesus with others and inviting them to give their lives to Him. The life she lived day in and day out, prior to, during, and now after all these hardships, is what has defined her legacy. She will forever be known and remembered by countless people for the heart she has for Jesus and the grace she used to walk through these days of extreme hardship.

This woman is one of the most incredible people I have ever met. She is my mother, and I am forever grateful to God for allowing me to be influenced by her guidance, faith, love, and support. I will be honest with you that even through the 22 surgeries, most of which were amputations, she continued to serve God and tell everyone she met about Jesus. My mom is one of the greatest examples I have ever seen of someone who is ridiculously legacy-minded. She walked through all of her pain, suffering, and hardships with legacy leverage in mind.

I remember how, one day, she leaned over to me and said, *"Nathan"*—only she and my father are allowed to call me by my real name—*"you know I have prayed to be able to have an impact in the lives of those who have gone through severe trauma and help give hope to those that have faced hardships and difficulties. Now those people can never say that I don't understand. One look at me, and they will know I understand what trauma is. If this all has happened so that the walls can be broken down and I can be a part of changing lives, then it is all worth it."*

This is heart, an incomparable amount of fuel, and her being completely locked in to the legacy she is here to leave. She has dedicated her entire life to helping others and giving them hope. She has walked through utter darkness, and her light has shone brighter than that of anyone else I have seen. She has dedicated herself to telling everyone she meets about Jesus and to giving them hope that their lives are meant to be so much more.

I can only hope and pray that my life leaves even a drop in the bucket compared to the legacy she has had and will leave behind. Watching her walk through this journey and still remain faithful to God and dedicated to supporting others has been life-changing for all who have witnessed it. Her faith and relationship with Jesus are what have kept her hopeful that what she has gone through will never be in vain and that God will use it to impact lives. These difficulties have only become the leverage she has used to build a greater legacy.

I know that my mother would want me to take a moment and plead with you to give your life to Jesus Christ. He has given you the opportunity to live in His grace and mercy, which is only available because of His sacrifice of laying down His life on the cross for you and me.

My father's leadership, faith, and obedience in following the biblical principles for our family were a cornerstone prior to the moments in the hospital, but they were even more solidified by his actions under extreme hardship. I am sure, in those moments, his mentality and conversation with God were similar to the story in Mark 9, where Jesus spoke to a father in desperation for his son. Jesus said to him, *"Everything is possible for one who believes."* The father replied, *"I do believe; help me overcome my unbelief."*

At all times, the reality of where we are must be acknowledged, and God can provide to bridge the gap in our weakness. I know my father would be the first to admit that in moments like these, we can ask in faith for a miracle, and at the same time, we are asking God to give us that very faith we need. I can't imagine the pressure on my father in those moments, stuck on the sidelines, unable to fix the situation. Despite the agony that he was in, he remained the foundation for my entire family. He sat with us, prayed with us, encouraged us, and even wept with us. His faith, actions, and leadership were incomparable and forever changed the perspective of those of us who walked through this with him.

The legacy my parents leave behind will not be based on the last years of their lives, but rather on the way they have shown their dedication to their lighthouse throughout the journey. Years ago, they set their sights on impact-based goals and ambitions, and they have followed through year after year to make them a reality.

As you can see from just this one life-changing circumstance, the journey has not been easy for them to bear. This was a major event with catastrophic outcomes, but it was only one of the many hardships and difficulties they faced during their lives. Their focus was constantly on the legacy they could leave behind, and they did not allow their feelings about the hardships to derail their purpose. They were dedicated to showing up daily and locked into building the momentum toward the lighthouse they identified. The daily movements they made were constantly taking the focused action steps required to carry out what they felt they were called to do.

This dedication and relentless spirit are great examples of the intersection of their lives, and they embody many other core principles we have worked through in this book. These are all vital in creating the legacy you are striving for. The fuel that drives you forward, the lighthouse that guides you, and who you are built to become are all part of your legacy. The life you are pursuing requires depth, purpose, and a conviction that goes beyond surface-level wants and needs. Those who find a greater purpose in life view every opportunity and their daily lives differently.

Simon Sinek, New York Times Best Selling Author, breaks it down in his own words: *"Most of us live our lives by accident—we live it as it happens. Fulfillment comes when we live our lives on purpose."* You cannot keep allowing your life to just happen or push through a life for the sake of living. The life worth creating is backed with purpose and focused on legacy.

Choose Your Living or Choose Your Legacy

Yes, your life is your own, and you are in full control of what actions you choose to take and which ones you choose not to. Neither I nor anyone else is here to take your freedom from you; rather, we are here to help you see the full potential of how you can maximize your freedoms to create your greatest future.

In most cases, I would beg you to break free from those cracked lenses that are hindering you from chasing after your future with freedom. All too many of us are living our lives with those expectations, pressures, and relational dynamics driving us to act and react in specific ways. This is one of the many hindering factors in our lives that can derail our progress and potential.

There is a question that we must confront: are we going to choose living or choose legacy? The key point here for your reflection is, what driver is pushing you to greater action? Your life has to be for more than just paying bills or getting a nicer car, a bigger house, or the newest watch to gain the approval of others. I am not saying any of these things are bad in themselves, but take the time to see your life beyond the stuff, beyond the requirements, and beyond the desire for others' approval. What could your life mean? What impact could you have during the days you have in front of you? What is the greatest story that you could create in your lifetime?

Of course, I need you to be able to pay your bills, but as you and I both know, you have the ability to control how much your bills are. I work with many people who make the excuse that they feel like they are stuck in the cycle of insanity because of their bills, but they refuse to make any decisions to lower their lifestyle and live in more cost-effective ways.

I have nothing against the great things in life, but you have to take into consideration that every time you say yes to the bigger things or the better things that cost more money, you are potentially saying no to more freedom. If you are focused on always having the newest and greatest, and this keeps you from having financial freedom, then you are saying yes to life and no to legacy.

I want to be very clear: I think having great things is great, and I love working hard so I can have fast cars, a nice house, and fishing boats and do lots of traveling. These things are all balanced with my greatest goals and ambitions, my lighthouse, in mind. I don't make any financial decisions that would create instability for my financial future and freedom. I keep my spending well below my income to remain completely flexible and adaptable to any adjustments in my legacy mission.

I am no different than you. I have those wants and always love the thought of a new ten-cylinder road machine, but I have to keep my wants in check with what I am choosing to chase after. I have worked extremely hard and am blessed by God to have financial freedom, but with the wrong focus and the domino effect of many bad decisions, I could put that in jeopardy.

This does not mean you have to live in a shack or never enjoy the finer things in life; rather, it is about keeping your priorities straight. I am not living my life to have lavish things; I am living my life to have great experiences with those I love, to build deep relationships with those who are near to me, and to create impact in this world of hurt. I am striving for my life to have meaning. When I leave this world, no one will remember the stuff I had, but I pray they are forever changed by the life I lived.

The decision to live a life focused on your legacy is not simple; it is a daily walk into a new way of life. The great part is that everything starts to look different, and every opportunity that is found or created seems to bring new life. In my current role, one of my favorite things I get to do is speaking, whether as a keynote speaker, an MC, or for company training. I love the opportunity to take people on a journey of connection through story, frameworks, laughter, tears, and even solemn moments.

Through each one, I ask God to allow me to impact at least one life, and for me, that is what legacy is about. I don't even care if they remember my name in five years; I only focus on being a part of their journey to break free from holdbacks and supporting them to take life-altering steps toward a greater future than they could ever have previously imagined.

I understand that right now you may feel stuck under the pressures of life and just hanging on. For some of you, it might even be that you are stuck in the broken-dreams mentality, where you can't see the other side of the hurt, hardship, and difficulties that you have faced. Others might be at the top of their success journey and don't want to take time away from chasing the mountain of success to reflect.

The truth that you will realize, either now or at a later point, is that there is no better time than now to refocus on legacy rather than just chasing after life. The life that you will feel is worth living has to be for more than just your conveniences, status, persona, and even survival at times. When you reflect and dial in your true ability to be a part of something greater than yourself, it allows you to focus on a purpose beyond just your own life or how you can bring light into the lives of others around you.

Let's make sure to clarify that I am not expecting you to quit your job, go on international missions, or donate all of your time to orphanages. There is a way to live your life on purpose and be intentional about having an impact while on your journey. This does require focus and even a decision to sacrifice at times, but living a life beyond just you creates a deeper joy than I could ever explain.

Each one of you has, or should have, your individualized vision of what your legacy could be. This is only found by locking into those core concepts we have covered: the displayed version of who you are capable of becoming, the fuel that is keeping you driven, and the lighthouse that is your guide.

I challenge you to reconnect to each of these and then reflect on what you are living for, either choosing life or choosing legacy. Then take that needed step back and ask yourself, how are your daily action steps lining up with the legacy that you want to leave? Never make the excuse that legacy is something you build later. You and I have not been promised the next day, only this day that we are living. We could be here today, and because of an accident, injury, or health-related hardship, we could be gone tomorrow.

I don't say all of this to scare you, but rather to connect you deeper to the realization that your legacy development is not something to wait on. The actions that you are taking every day and the momentum you are building should all be legacy-driven and lighthouse-focused.

Heads Up or Heads Down

There are those moments when you feel like your world may be crumbling all around you. The times when you feel like the beatings just won't stop, and you can't seem to catch your breath. It becomes a natural reaction to get stuck, look down at the circumstances you are facing, and lick your wounds. This often goes even further into the "why me" mentality, and others sulk in disbelief.

I am not going to tell you that when you are in those tough times and trials in your life, sitting in the moment of "what is going on" shouldn't be a normal first reaction. It is understandable that it can be very overwhelming, difficult, and straight-up frustrating and disheartening when the hardships keep coming or catastrophic events occur. What I have identified as the most important next step is figuring out how you are going to control your long-term perspective on these situations. Yes, it is easiest to stay in the initial reaction or even move into bitterness and the "it's not fair" mentality. This is why we have to have a greater reason beyond just ourselves or this phase of our lives to shake up our mindset and perspective.

The heads-down mentality is looking at situations and focusing on what has occurred and how it has messed up your plans, outcomes, or situations in your life. It is so natural to want to lick your wounds and stay in this self-focused mentality rather than placing the requirement on yourself to look at it all from a different angle or vantage point.

This is why having your lighthouse locked in and a legacy mindset as your focus becomes vital. This allows you to walk through circumstances and hardships with the perspective shift of how you can leverage each to maximize your momentum or impact others. This is not only a great reflection point, but it can also be the light that helps you walk through difficult times of darkness.

As I expressed in Chapter Five, a major hope that I clung to during my darkest times was the fact that I needed to push through in order to be able to help others find their way in their darkest hours. No one is going to judge you for taking time to put your head down and focus while working through the initial phases of the challenges you face. That season is often necessary. However, you cannot allow yourself to stay there. Your future requires a different approach, one that lifts your eyes and keeps you focused on the lighthouse you've set for your life.

When you are locked in with your head up and connected to the goals and ambitions layered within that lighthouse, hardships become nothing more than bumps in the road. Without a long-term, greater purpose guiding your perspective, it's easy to get stuck every time difficulty arises. A heads-up approach allows you to identify the lessons within every situation you encounter, equipping you to move forward with clarity and relentless momentum.

It's vital to remember that everything you face provides experiences that cannot be otherwise earned, achieved, or purchased. These moments are building your foundation and expanding your toolbox for the journey ahead. Every roadblock and detour presents an opportunity to learn, grow, and leverage, especially when your perspective extends beyond just yourself.

Amberly Lago, USA Today Top Influential Speaker, Best-Selling Author, Global Top 1% Podcast Host, lays this out in a way that is connective and deep:

Every challenge, every hard thing that we go through helps prepare us, develops that grit in us and that resilience in us... although I don't ever wish for some of the hard things that I went through as a kid, like abuse, and not the safest home growing up. But with those things, I've been able to help others walk and navigate their way through those challenges.

Having your legacy locked in and a part of your lighthouse allows you to keep your eyes set on your greater life and brings a redemptive perspective in the midst of your most difficult times.

Defined and Deliberate

For some of you, the statement "Your legacy is waiting" is directly connected to the root of defining what your legacy is meant to be. You are stuck playing it safe, never willing to set your eyes on what your life could become if you pushed yourself to your full potential. There is a bigger version of who you have been built to become and the legacy you could create that needs to be put into motion.

Even with fears, holdbacks, and resistances, defining what you have been built to take on and the impact you are driven to have gives a bigger purpose. The pain of the fears, holdbacks, and resistances will be outweighed by the drive, passion, and desire to create your legacy. You are left with the option to push through and take focused action or, alternatively, allow yourself to squander the opportunity in front of you. The life you live is your only chance to write your story, create a meaningful impact, and build your legacy. There are no do-overs, rewrites, or takebacks when you are facing your last breath.

I know this is serious, and for some of you, it might be something you avoid thinking about or discussing. You have to connect to the seriousness of this and determine if you are going to be deliberate about your actions and how they connect to the defined legacy you are striving to live for. The past cannot be your excuse, and your failures do not define your life. Connecting to your purpose, mission, and dreams, then taking the life-changing action steps daily, is what is required.

Intentionality with your actions builds the momentum in your life toward where you place deliberate focus. The legacy you have locked in for your life will require this type of dedication and you being determined to never quit or give up. The achievement of building your life toward your legacy is not something that comes easily or by accident. There is a need for you to dig deep with grit and resilience to keep yourself navigating correctly and propelled forward.

Having your intentions set in place and the outcomes that you are chasing after clear and concise is of the utmost importance. You will never know what it is like to build your greatest outcome unless you are deliberate in identifying and building the legacy that could be your future.

One Question, Forever Changed

What are the dreams you never knew could be yours? The haunting effect of this one question I asked myself during my own reflection years ago was a huge influence on me in writing this entire book. As I worked through this, I determined that all the programming and cracked lenses from my past were completely convoluting my ability to see my potential and future. I looked at other people's ability to create better lives and thought it was only available to specific people. I never knew I could have dreams of greatness. I struggled to dream of any life I could create that would be of great meaning. I was stuck with a limitation in my ability to dream or cast a greater vision for my life, left assuming nothing great would ever be within my reach.

After working through the major holdbacks in my life and navigating many limiting beliefs and false perspectives, I was able to reframe my past and create the first dream for my future. Think about this as version 1.0, and I realized very quickly that it still had limitations and remnants of the cracked lenses that were deeply rooted. I have had to do constant work to push past these resistances and reprogram my belief system to fully connect with and believe all that I am capable of.

The life I am living now is greater than I could have imagined, and the development of my dreams continues to grow and become even more extravagant. The legacy I am striving for goes beyond me and my family; it is focused on bringing hope to as many individuals as I can reach and working to connect them to their greater purpose.

All too many people have given up; they have lost hope for the life they are able to create. The truth, though, is that they have only begun the process of their development and have allowed their inability to see their life for what it truly can become to drive their inaction. This is why I am focused on you understanding that your dreams don't have to be broken and your life can be greater than you could have ever previously imagined.

The effects of cracked lenses and programming from your early life create barriers and limitations that can be destructive to your ability to dream your greatest dreams. I am not talking about butterflies, rainbows, and unicorns, but rather about your ability to see a true vision of what your life could become if you became fully intentional, locked into your purpose, and relentless in the face of all obstacles. What could your life really look like if you released all the internal holdbacks, expectations from others, outside pressures, and even your fears and insecurities?

Yes, I want you to get a little carried away with your dreaming. I want you to unleash the inner dreamer that can think about a greater life for yourself and create an impact or legacy that will last beyond the days you live.

I am constantly revisiting and challenging my dreams and pushing myself to see beyond what I have previously laid out. This is why, earlier in this book, I encouraged you to challenge your dreams and even challenge everything you know. Just because it is something you know or have known doesn't mean it is right or right for you.

There are many things in my life and in the lives of my clients that should have been challenged early on in our adult lives but were normalized within our programming and affected how we pursued life. I am not saying to put an anchor in the sand in every area of your life and start working through every belief system and expected action, but rather, as you continue to take action, unlock that "inner two-year-old" to ask why. Uncover the roots of these beliefs, understandings, perspectives, resistances, expectations, and limitations.

I know that as you become clearer about your long-term dreams, some resistance can arise due to your current capabilities, abilities, and even opportunities. Remember, the person you are today is not capable of achieving the goals and ambitions you are laying out. You are not currently good enough, connected enough, or even skilled enough to accomplish all that you should be setting out to achieve. The dreams you are creating should make you a bit nervous, and you should fully understand that achieving them will require you to become more dedicated, disciplined, and growth-oriented than ever before. Only by compounding growth and development each day will you be able to see your dreams come to full fruition.

If what your dreams are made of is something you can currently achieve, then they are restrictive and greatly limited. Your dreams should be almost completely out of reach but in line with your purpose, abilities, skill sets, and natural gifts.

I would encourage you to reflect on this question, which remains part of my personal process each year. What are the dreams you never knew could be yours? Truly sit in and reflect on this and work back through the displayed version of who you are capable of becoming and what you could take on in your life, overcome, and accomplish. Remove the limitations and lock into the legacy that's waiting for you.

Missing in Action

Imagine an action movie where the hero is busy sulking over their fears, insecurities, and misconceptions about what they could take on. They seclude themselves in their own comfort, leaving those in need to their demise.

Now think about real-life situations that have happened: the heroes who showed up and stood up for what they believed in or who sacrificed themselves to save others. What if these people had let their limiting beliefs overtake them in those moments and then failed to take action? What about good ol' George Washington? What if he allowed his thoughts of being only a mere man to get to him? Would he have ever led the patriot forces to victory, allowing us to have freedom? What about Martin Luther King Jr.? What if he had allowed the noise surrounding him and the limitations placed upon people of color to keep him from speaking up? What would our lives be like today without that great voice and leadership?

I can give you countless examples of those who pushed beyond what their pasts, expectations, and even constricting beliefs would have told them was within acceptable limits. If these people had allowed those distractions and limiting beliefs to overtake them, the legacy they created would never have been established. What if any of these were "missing in action" in their lives because they drew back rather than charging forward with the right actions?

You might not think of yourself as a hero or someone who could be the catalyst for change, but I guarantee you that many of those who have taken great faith steps in their lives had those moments, days, and even almost their entire lives believing that they were not capable of creating the change that they did. This is why you cannot be missing in action in the story of your life and fail to take the necessary steps to pursue your legacy.

You are here for an incredible purpose, and it requires you to lock into what that is and how you are to leverage who you are to create greater change, more focused impact, or your greatest outcome. You cannot stay hidden under a rock or stand by, waiting for others to step up and bridge the gap in your life. You have a responsibility not just to yourself but to those who surround you to live as the example of what overcoming obstacles, difficulties, and hardships can look like.

This overcoming is not so you can pump your chest and gain the attention of onlookers, but to be the beam of light where others can find hope that there is a potential for a better life. What has been is not what defines you. What you do today and how you choose to show up from here on out is what creates the legacy of your life.

Walking through your life with a perspective of what all you can gain, earn, and obtain is a self-focused perspective. This is not just about stuff and money but also about attention, fame, and approval from others. What could be missing in your life is a deeper purpose and greater aspirations that go beyond what you can do for yourself.

Yes, there is the perspective that we have to first put on our own oxygen mask before we can help others. I fully agree that we should first find our own way and have a history of overcoming before we guide others on their journey, but the intentionality of each step looks very different when you are internally rather than externally focused. When you focus on being the light in the darkness for others on their own journey, your openness about your struggles, difficulties, and even failures becomes apparent.

Your legacy is waiting for you, and you have to reflect on and identify what is missing in your life. Have you done the required work to lock into the displayed version of yourself and what you've built to take on and accomplish in your life? Are you connected to the heart fuel that is driving you? Have you clearly defined and created the lighthouse that you are staying focused on with all your actions and momentum?

Your legacy is built by the days you live, by your ability to remain focused despite what is going on around you. Don't let your story be one where the hero chooses to sit on the sidelines and give power to complacency, the past, limiting beliefs, and other holdbacks. Becoming the person capable of creating a legacy of impact and change requires hard work, dedication, and taking action when all others are resistant.

The opportunity in front of you is based on the dedication you place in overcoming the cracked lenses, limiting beliefs, and false truths that you have allowed to shape the way you see yourself, your potential, and your future. You have to break free from these holdbacks and chase after the dreams you are capable of creating. You cannot allow your dreams to be broken because of your refusal to do the hard work and fully identify the core truth of what your life could become. You cannot be missing in action in the legacy that is created by your purpose, your actions, and your life.

Rewrite, Reset, Reclaim

When you take a step back and look at life, a bit of craziness comes into view. Think about it; there is no playbook or exact roadmap for the individualized journey that you are on. Each of us has worked through aspects of our lives, doing our best to remain sane and not completely lose it as we strive to gain traction and achieve a greater life.

Then you have those people called parents, who attempt to do all of this and raise children, some of whom are more challenging than others, without failing them in a grave manner. Those children grow up and follow in the footsteps and guidance of the people who raised them, and then you add in their own mistakes and issues that they create. This is a domino effect of issues that keeps going until someone decides to question and challenge aspects of this entire cycle to determine an approach to identify and create change in their own journey.

I am not talking about a teenage rebellion but rather a mature approach, as an adult, to working through and challenging the things you heard, saw, experienced, and were taught throughout your childhood. It is always important to remember that just because it was, it doesn't mean it is what should be.

Also, you have to consider that broken people raise broken people. I am not saying that you are falling apart or that you have parents who are utterly broken. I am working to put into perspective the fact that the generations that have come before us all had different fears, concerns, ways of handling matters, priorities, and so many other factors at hand. Consider how many people don't take the time to fully understand all the whys behind what they heard or were taught, but just continue with those same factors at hand and even pass them down to the next generation.

I have seen highly intelligent and academically promising individuals refuse to attend college because their father instilled in them the belief that they were destined to turn a wrench. I have worked with many women who, despite having a thriving career, felt like they were constantly failing because they were not the ones cleaning the house or doing the laundry. They were programmed by their parents and even grandparents to quantify success as a woman through their activities related to the home.

I have worked with struggling entrepreneurs who have never felt good enough, despite great success, because their parents demanded they attend law school, and they refused. I could provide a multitude of examples of people whose childhoods created a form of derailment in their progress or the future they could have had because of the way things were communicated, examples that were seen, or the demands placed on them.

In each of our lives, there has to be a point at which we challenge and question what we know, what is expected of us, and how we look at our future and potential. The great part about growth and maturity is the ability to use our discernment to work back through these very things and uncover the truth. I explained the technique earlier in this book, but I need you to know that just because I call it the "inner two-year-old," this doesn't mean there's a lack of maturity in the process. This is just an easy way to remember the need to constantly ask about the "why" behind your behaviors, beliefs, habits, automatic responses, natural draws, and almost every other aspect of your decision-making and processing.

This technique has saved me a lot of frustration, failed turns, and derailing actions, but most people don't take the time to step back and ask why. This has also been part of my ability to connect with dreams I never knew could be mine. Without working through these factors in my life and recognizing that my parents could have had their own cracked lenses that may have created cracks in mine, I would never have been able to pursue many of the things I have accomplished.

When you realize that we are all working through life and handling each step to the best of our abilities, it opens the door to connect with our childhood with the understanding that, even in the best of circumstances and with parental role models, we are all still a bit broken. I am not saying your parents failed you, and as you work through this, it is not an opportunity to cast blame or judgment but rather to lock into the ownership that you are in control of each next step in your life. Now that I have broken down and laid out the processes and action steps, it is up to you to create your momentum and never let your dreams break.

Rewrite Your Story

The past cannot be changed, which leaves you with a hard decision. Are you going to allow the past to be what defines your future, or are you going to rewrite your story and create the narrative of overcoming odds and uncovering greatness?

Recognizing the cracked lenses that are present in your life that distort the way you see yourself and your potential is pivotal as you work to create and chase your dreams. Working through your past and identifying circumstances, situations, and statements that created the cracks is the initial step, followed by the required reframing with your more mature vantage point.

The trajectory of your story up to this moment does not control the outcome of how your story will unfold. You are the only current author of your story; those who have controlled any aspects in the past are no longer able to dictate or determine the next step or the end result. This is also true if, during your authorship, you have created many self-inflicted wounds and what some would consider a scene of immense despair. The actions of your past and the decisions you have made are not what define you; it is the actions that you take from this moment on.

The encouraging part about this is that, in every failure, hardship, and even those complete clusters that we find ourselves in or create, it is not the end. The next steps we take and how we handle rising from the darkness or difficulty determine how we will be remembered. The story for your life and for mine cannot be left in those moments of despair; we have to take control of this moment, our mindset, and our next focused step.

As a part of the encouragement I want to leave you with here at the end of this book, I will give you a clear and concise three-step process to move quickly through the past situations, circumstances, or other factors that may have created cracked lenses.

The first step is to reflect, which is to work back into your past with the purpose of identifying why you are pulled in a specific direction, why you are viewing yourself in a specific light, why you are struggling to see the potential of your great dreams, or other ways you are being held back.

Once you identify the situation, statement, or other factor, move to the second step: the reframe. We pushed deep into this in Chapter Five, but the most important aspect here is to go back with the more mature lens and connect to the truth behind what was said, done, or occurred. Connecting differently to these situations and using the "inner two-year-old" to investigate the "why" at every angle leaves you with more clarity about the misconceptions and convoluted perspectives you previously allowed to control your actions.

The last step in this process is to redefine, taking all of this from the past and creating a new definition of what truth is. Many times, when we work back, there are truths that we have clung to about what we need to do with our lives, our limitations, and the directions we should take and avoid. Redefining what truth is allows us to break free from the things holding us back. The freedom that comes with these three impactful steps allows us to take full advantage of new actions that are laying the foundation for the story that we choose to write.

Reset Your Identity

The concept of identity is a complex topic, as there are many ways people define their identity or advise others on how to form it. There have been multiple psychological studies that have many perspectives on how identity is formed, and unfortunately, there are too many approaches for this determination to give anyone a clear answer. This leaves some questions to confront in your life: What is your current identity defined by? What are you holding onto that is building your identity or self-worth? What are you allowing to influence your identity? Who are you allowing to shape how you view your identity?

These questions help you push through and wrestle with many issues that most people struggle with throughout their lives. I understand that this can leave you in a bit of a frustrating cycle of insanity if you're not careful. That is why I need to push you to lock into something greater than just whatever you define as your identity for today. This is why, throughout this book, I have challenged you to create the displayed version of the greatest you that is possible. In Chapter Six, I pushed you to dive deep into the core aspects of who you are, based on your skill set, abilities, and capabilities.

These, coupled with your natural bent and the ongoing development of who you are capable of becoming, should be what you hold true to. The only definition of who you are and your identity should be completely based on you and have nothing to do with outside factors. Then, using all this information and the growth and development you are capable of, you can create a display of who you can become and what you can take on in your life.

When you truly work through all of this, connecting with your passions and areas of purpose, it allows you to start working toward your legacy. This is where things get interesting, and the concept of identity becomes less important as legacy becomes the driving factor.

I have hit hard on the importance of legacy, and I will save you all the continuation of that soapbox, but walking you through this felt like an important aspect not to bypass. The legacy you leave behind is the most important identity that you will ever have. Being known for a specific action, outcome, or other factor is minuscule compared to your ability to leave a legacy through the constant actions you take in connection with your purpose.

Reclaim Your Future

The incredible news for you and me is that we are still here. We still have this day. God has allowed us to breathe another day and continue living the blessed life we have. There is no doubt that many of you are facing hardships and difficulties, but even in the midst of them, your life is still a blessing.

This is where you have decisions to make and perspectives to confront. I can't walk you through every day and keep your head up when you feel the storms are all around, but I will call you out on the focus that you put into your difficulties. Life isn't going to be easy, but you get to control what you learn and take away from every situation that you come across. The benefit of going through hardships is the ability to learn lessons that cannot be bought or taught and to add new abilities to your toolbox that can be leveraged to impact lives. This is a huge part of reclaiming your future: the ability to redeem those tough situations, faceplants, and even self-inflicted wounds. Your future is defined by your actions and created by your intentional dedication to continue moving toward your legacy and lighthouse.

This is where, in your current day, you must be driven by that deep-rooted fuel, locked in and focused toward building momentum on the journey to reach your lighthouse. You have to walk away from all the excuses that are keeping you bound and held back. Your life is right in front of you, and the future that you have the ability to create will be an incredible example for others if you set determination in motion.

I can take all I want for you and couple it with my drive and ambition, but it will not get you anywhere. Your future is personal; you are required to participate fully to reclaim a new future for yourself. You cannot allow your dreams to be shattered by the cracked lenses in your life. You cannot allow the tides that push and pull to derail your actions. The life that you are reclaiming for yourself is worth the battle. I have never and will never tell you that this journey is easy, but the results are rewarding.

Reclaiming means fighting to take something back that was rightfully yours. This is all about you putting focused effort into redefining who you are based on truth and redeveloping the potential that you have based on the facts of how you have been built. Yes, it requires you to confront those things that you heard, saw, dealt with, and even created in yourself. This is why I consider it a true fight; the work is deep, and the effort required is great. You have to have the right fuel locked in and a deep-rooted connection to the source.

Many push through life, never doing the work required to break free from these holdbacks, and end up with failed attempts or derailed progress. My hope for you is that you will be eager and ready to confront those issues from the past and drive forward as a force to reclaim the life you were built to create.

Delayed but Never Broken

As this book comes to a close, I feel it is important to make sure you know that this is not the end but your new beginning. I didn't write this book to be your cheerleader; I wrote this to be a guide on your journey. My heart is for you to be able to reconnect with the dreams you once knew, develop them, and create new ones you never knew could be yours.

It is tough for people like you and me to look back and see what we consider wasted time, but you have to keep the vantage point that this was all a journey to get to this moment. This is why I need you, or better yet, you need yourself, to lock into the dedication to never again allow your dreams to be broken. I guarantee you that if you are anything like me, then the regrets of failures will haunt you. The way I cope is by understanding that, in those moments, I hadn't yet gained the knowledge to know better.

At this point, I have laid out the principles I use to create life-changing experiences for my clients as clearly as I know how. I don't want you to leave this moment with any excuses, which means your future regrets are all on you. You cannot continue to allow your cracked lenses to dictate your outcomes; your actions must be focused and aligned with your lighthouse.

This might sound harsh, but if you read this book for entertainment, then I am not sure it met your expectations. This book has been developed as a detailed source of solutions to ensure you are given the proper tools, processes, and even connective stories to support you on your journey.

This next phase of your life will serve as a defining moment, revealing your grit, resilience, and commitment to focused action. I implore you to work through the principles again and identify all the application points most relevant to your life. Daily movements and momentum are required to build the progress toward your lighthouse, but you must have all the core aspects dialed in to ensure your dreams will never be broken.

The life in front of you is filled with potential, opportunities, impact, and unlimited possibilities, but you have to do the work to build the foundation required to launch into your greatest direction. There is no doubt that there have been delays in the fulfillment of your dreams. Your future demands that you dig deep, push hard, and even battle relentlessly to ensure your dreams are never broken.

THANK YOU FOR READING MY BOOK!

I am hoping that this book has had an impact on your life and will forever change the way you see yourself, your future, and your full potential. My entire goal for this book was to be a part of the change that is needed for you to see a new perspective and to have the greatest future you are capable of achieving. Writing this book has required me to push deep into some of my hardest days and connect back to those moments where I felt hopeless. I am praying that through my openness and vulnerability, you are able to connect to your ability to write your own story and chase after your dreams.

The following section of this book is the bonus content that has been put together with the help of all the participants who are shown. This has been an enjoyable project to work on, and I know this will have an impact on your life.

Thank you for all your love and support.

I would appreciate it if you could leave your invaluable review on Amazon.com with your feedback. Thank you!

BONUS CONTENT
Connection & Encouragement

This bonus section of the book has been developed with the joint participation of all the incredible individuals listed on the following pages. Each of these great individuals has participated with a heart of having an impact on your life. They each are focused on helping you build hope through the connection to their life stories and difficulties, as well as encouragement from their pathway of overcoming obstacles. Please take the time to read through the quotes, encouragements, and challenges from each of these great individuals. Get access to all of their full interviews, which are available for you to watch on the resources page, use the QR Code below, or go to www.CrackedLensesBook.com/Resources.

Disclaimer: Included on the following pages are exact quotes from these individuals, but there are also summarized aspects and small adjustments to assist with clarity of messaging and the required editing from conversational format to written format. I have worked to keep the heart of all of their quotes, encouragements for you, and challenges in line with how they communicated them in the interviews. I strongly encourage you to watch or listen to the full interview of each individual for the highest level of impact.

Amberly Lago

USA Today Top Influential Speaker, Best-Selling Author,
Global Top 1% Podcast Host

Amberly Lago is an internationally recognized motivational speaker, USA Today *Top Influential Speaker*, best-selling author, and resilience coach. Known for her energy, authenticity, and powerful storytelling, Amberly delivers transformative messages that move audiences to action.

At 38 years old, Amberly's life changed forever after a devastating motorcycle accident that resulted in 34 surgeries and a long journey through chronic pain, depression, and self-doubt. Rather than allowing her circumstances to define her, she chose to rise—transforming adversity into a platform for impact.

Amberly is the author of *True Grit & Grace* and *Joy Through the Journey* and the host of *The Amberly Lago Show*, where she shares conversations centered on resilience, leadership, mindset, and wholehearted living. Through keynotes, coaching, and media appearances, she empowers audiences to overcome obstacles, lead with courage, and create meaningful lives fueled by purpose and joy.

Impactful Quote from the Interview:

"I think every challenge and every hard thing that we go through helps prepare us and develops that grit in us and that resilience in us. And although I don't ever wish for some of the hard things that I went through as a kid, like abuse and not having the safest home growing up, because of those things, I've been able to help others walk and navigate their way through those challenges."

Encouragement for You from the Interview:

When life feels heavy or confusing, come back to trusting your gut. Many of us were taught, often by people we were supposed to trust, to ignore our instincts, but our gut never lies. Your head may overthink, and your heart may feel torn, yet your inner knowing recognizes when something is off and when something is aligned. In hard seasons, clarity comes from anchoring to your values and paying attention to energy—what drains you versus what restores you. Difficulty doesn't mean you're lost; it often means you're being invited back to yourself.

Challenge for You from the Interview:

One powerful step toward healing and growth is taking an honest look at who you're surrounding yourself with. The people you allow into your life, both in person and through social media, have a real impact on your choices, mindset, and momentum. Growth sometimes requires letting go of relationships or influences that keep you stuck in old patterns or negativity, even when that decision is uncomfortable. Choosing better for yourself often starts with choosing environments and people that support the direction you're committed to moving.

Here are the best places for you to learn more about Amberly Lago:

Follow the QR code to the Resources Page, where you can watch the entire interview

Website: www.AmberlyLago.com

Follow on Instagram: @amberlylagomotivation

Ben Newman

USA Today Top 5 Coach in the World, TOP 50 Keynote Speaker,
2x Wall Street Journal Best Seller

Ben Newman is a globally respected performance coach, keynote speaker, and 2× Wall Street Journal best-selling author who helps leaders, athletes, and organizations unlock sustained excellence through mental toughness, discipline, and intentional focus. Recognized by *USA Today* as one of the Top 5 Mindset & Performance Coaches in the World, Ben has spent decades working alongside elite athletes, championship teams, Fortune 500 companies, and high-performing executives to build cultures rooted in accountability and purpose.

Before becoming a performance coach, Ben was a top 2% financial advisor, an experience that shaped his practical, results-driven approach to leadership and performance. His work has impacted organizations and athletes across the NFL, NBA, MLB, PGA, UFC, NCAA, and multiple Super Bowl-winning teams. As the host of *The Burn Podcast* and author of books including *Uncommon Leadership* and *The Standard*, Ben challenges people to identify their "Burn," the deeper reason that fuels resilience, consistency, and long-term impact. Through his coaching and speaking, he empowers others to eliminate fear-based thinking, raise their standards, and commit to the long game of uncommon success.

Impactful Quote from the Interview:

"The secret of the highest performers is that they understand that burn that ignites their why and purpose. It causes them to show up on the days they don't feel like it, and especially after they win. So through my mother's words,

her journal, and her example, there's this burn inside of me. Knowing that my mother died at 38 and I'm 46, that's eight extra years she never got; you better dang well believe I'm going to attack every day.

It's also the opportunity to now help others find their burn and find what their deep-rooted story is, the sacrifice that they want to make, or how they want to honor the sacrifice that's been made for them."

Encouragement for You from the Interview:

I would encourage others to have faith sooner and know they don't have to do life on their own. I resisted spirituality when I was younger, but finding Christ later brought a deeper sense of support, purpose, and peace. Even though I wish I had discovered that relationship earlier, I also believe it came at the right time and led to incredible growth.

Challenge for You from the Interview:

Silence the negative self-talk. Silence the noise. Have an honest conversation with yourself after hearing the story I share. And ask yourself, what am I holding on to? Or what am I seeking approval for? Look in that mirror of accountability; honestly, find the courage, find the honesty in yourself, and have the strength to just let it go… And if you can do that, and you can accept that challenge, my hope and my prayer would be that you don't wait decades the way that I did; you take care of it now.

Here are the best places for you to learn more about Ben Newman:

Follow the QR code to the Resources Page,
where you can watch the entire interview
Website: www.BenNewman.net
Follow on Instagram: @ContinuedFight

Brad Bosh

Farm Bureau Regional Vice Pres., State of the Year
& Chairman's Challenge Award Recipient

Brad Bosh is a Regional Vice President for South Dakota at Farm Bureau Financial Services, bringing more than 21 years of experience in the financial services industry. Over the course of his career, Brad spent 17 years as a Hall of Fame Agent and later served as a District Manager before stepping into regional leadership. Under his direction, South Dakota was recognized as *State of the Year* in 2025, reflecting sustained performance, strong client relationships, and a results-driven culture. His team also earned the Chairman's Challenge award in both 2024 and 2025 for achieving the highest year-over-year percentage growth in life and annuity sales.

A Chartered Financial Consultant (ChFC), Brad is known for blending technical expertise with a people-first approach to leadership. He is deeply committed to developing leaders, strengthening processes, and aligning strategy with frontline execution to drive ethical, sustainable growth. Focused on talent development and disciplined execution, Brad helps build high-performing teams that deliver long-term value for clients and communities. Grounded in servant leadership, he believes lasting success is built through clarity, consistency, and investing in people, principles shaped by his faith, his family, and his commitment to community.

Impactful Quote from the Interview:

"You can't get distracted by the outside noise. You can't be distracted by what people think of you or who they think you are. Those people don't even know you. You can't allow yourself to get caught up in the weeds with what people

are saying about you.… You know who you are; be true to you and push through with a chip on your shoulder to prove them all wrong."

Encouragement for You from the Interview:

You have to face your storms head-on. Tiptoeing around problems doesn't make them go away—it only prolongs them. Growth comes from going straight at the challenge, moving through it, and trusting you'll be better on the other side. While some hardships can't be predicted or avoided, many work-related challenges can be addressed immediately. If there's a problem, handle it directly and with respect, rather than letting it linger. Dealing with issues head-on frees your mind, strengthens relationships, and leaves everyone better for it in the end.

Challenge for You from the Interview:

Chasing goals matters, but so does leaving things better than you found them. Strive to win, aim to be the best, and embrace the challenge, but don't lose sight of relationships along the way. Lead as a human being, not a corporate version of yourself, and give people real answers, not rehearsed ones. Be true to who you are, because authenticity goes a long way in work, in leadership, and in life. People respond to consistency and honesty, and when you show up the same way everywhere, you build trust, connection, and impact that lasts beyond the goal itself.

Here are the best places for you to learn more about Brad Bosh:

Follow the QR code to the Resources Page, where you can watch the entire interview.
Follow on LinkedIn: @Brad Bosh, CHFC

Chris Welton

Renowned Performance Coach, Best-Selling Author, TEDx Speaker

Chris Welton is a dynamic speaker, performance coach, TEDx presenter, and international best-selling author with over 30 years of experience in leadership and sales. Born with one hand, Chris transformed personal adversity into a life mission rooted in responsibility, faith, and intentional living. His journey shaped a message that challenges people to stop drifting, take ownership of their choices, and live with clarity and conviction.

Through speaking engagements, coaching, and his *One Hand At A Time* podcast, Chris equips individuals and organizations to build resilience, discipline, and purpose from the inside out. Known for his honest, relatable approach, he helps people align their lives with what truly matters, reminding them that meaningful change doesn't happen by accident but through conscious decisions made one step, and one day, at a time.

Impactful Quote from the Interview:

"There's no easy button in life if you want to be great. If you're chasing greatness and you're trying to be an incredible leader or father or whatever, it's not a fixed target. It's something that you have to keep chasing. It just keeps moving; you have to keep going after it, evolving to be bigger and better, faster, stronger, whatever that is to get there."

Encouragement for You from the Interview:

Don't want to go back and change anything in your past, because every hardship shaped who you are today, the genuine person you've become. If things had been easier or if you'd known they would get better sooner, you might not have done the work or grown the way you did. The struggle mattered because some lessons can't be given; they have to be lived.

Challenge for You from the Interview:

Challenge yourself to believe in what you truly want. Create a clear vision for where you're going next, regardless of your past or how you feel about the future, and choose to believe it's possible. Belief is powerful; when you believe you can become something or accomplish something, your chances increase dramatically. Without your belief in yourself, the odds are against you.

Here are the best places for you to learn more about Chris Welton:

Follow the QR code to the Resources Page,
where you can watch the entire interview
Website: www.ChrisWelton.Live
Follow on Instagram: @OneHandataTime

Drew Davis

Keynote Speaker, Certified Coach, Former NFL & Collegiate Athlete

Drew Davis is a speaker, certified coach, and entrepreneur who helps individuals break free from limiting patterns and step into lives of clarity, confidence, and purpose. A former NFL wide receiver and collegiate athlete, Drew's journey through high-level sports, setbacks, and transition beyond the game shaped his grounded, relatable message around mindset, identity, and personal responsibility. His experiences taught him that success isn't just about talent or performance but about belief, discipline, and intentional choices.

Through speaking engagements, coaching, and digital platforms, Drew equips audiences with practical tools to strengthen belief, create vision, and move forward with consistency. Known for his authentic, action-oriented approach, he helps people align who they are with where they're going, empowering them to lead themselves well, navigate transition, and build meaningful progress in both life and business.

Impactful Quote from the Interview:

"Stay ready; that way, you don't have to get ready. I'm going to be locked and loaded, ready to go. What makes life, life is that you never know where that breakthrough is going to happen…. You don't know when that breakthrough is going to be. But if you quit, you walk away, you give up, you definitely will never see it because you didn't continue going until you reached the end…. Nothing that's easy is worth having."

Encouragement for You from the Interview:

You have to find different ways to get it done. Your plan A might not work, but you have to keep working and pushing, even if it is all the way to plan Z. The tenacity, the energy, and the focus that you hit things with matter. It's going to pay off. Never be defined by the box that you are put into or what career you choose to chase after; always continue to work on yourself.

Challenge for You from the Interview:

Practice being uncomfortably comfortable. That means doing things you're not used to and living a little outside the box. If you're going to the third floor, take the stairs. If you're really good with one hand, try using the other one sometimes. Do small things that stretch you. Keep choosing the things that make you uncomfortable, because that's where growth happens.

Step into that space without needing to be complete or fully formed. Give yourself permission to grow, to learn, to fail, to come back, and to try again. Too often, we start something, struggle at first, and decide we're just not good at it, when really, with a growth mindset, it's something we can work on and improve. So keep practicing being uncomfortably comfortable in the things you want to pursue, and give yourself the space to not know yet, to figure it out, and to discover what you're good at and what the next phase of your life is meant to be.

Here are the best places for you to learn more about Drew Davis:

Follow the QR code to the Resources Page,
where you can watch the entire interview
Website: www.DrewJayDavis.com
Follow on Instagram: @DrewJayDavis

Jaime Elizondo

Certified High-Performance Coach, Best-Selling Author,
Former NFL & CFL Head Coach

Jaime Elizondo is a Certified High-Performance Coach, international speaker, and best-selling author with over 25 years of leadership experience shaped by elite-level football and performance development. A seasoned head coach in both the National Football League (NFL) and the Canadian Football League (CFL), Jaime's career includes impactful roles with the New Orleans Saints and New England Patriots in the NFL and a Grey Cup championship as offensive coordinator of the Ottawa Redblacks. He also served as head coach, offensive coordinator, and quarterbacks coach for the Edmonton Elks in the CFL, bringing strategic vision and player development expertise to every team he led.

Today, Jaime combines his deep understanding of high-stakes performance with cutting-edge neuroscience, coaching, and psychology to guide individuals, teams, and organizations from high potential to elite performance. As the creator of the transformative CRUSH-It and ICE frameworks, he guides audiences toward resilience, clarity, leadership, and meaningful growth, helping people not just dream but perform with intention, courage, and consistency.

Impactful Quote from the Interview:

"Those limiting beliefs really start to work in your subconscious, that you're not good enough, that you're not destined for more, that you're not capable of greatness, and so I think the choice is when we choose to focus on those and listen to those. It haunted me with my unconscious behaviors, and by having

this identity that had been attached to me from adolescence, I had to prove that I belonged. At every stop along the way, my focus was on proving that I belonged, and that served me in some capacities, but in others, it hurt me because instead of focusing on building the team, building the coaching staff, and building and integrating myself effectively into the existing culture, I was trying to prove that I belonged. So in the early stages of my career, it held me back, because I always felt I had something to prove."

Encouragement for You from the Interview:

I would encourage the younger version of myself and others to be less focused on themselves, because self-centeredness often turns into self-consciousness, comparison, and eventually judgment. Greater self-awareness in the moment is what leads to real growth. Rather than fixating on your own track or career, focus on helping others and the impact you can have, because when service becomes the starting point, growth and fulfillment follow naturally.

Challenge for You from the Interview:

There are three things I would challenge people to focus on. First, you have to intentionally craft the identity you want, and that often means going deep and answering some difficult questions about yourself. In life, there are only a few moments when the mirror shows up, those key juncture points where you get to choose which path you're going to take. If you don't have awareness, you miss them. Awareness is what allows you to recognize this is one of those moments and choose intentionally.

Second, discipline is everything. That includes the discipline to regulate your emotions, your mind, and your thinking, as well as the discipline to do the hard physical things that drive performance. But it starts mentally and emotionally. Third, consistency is what truly separates those who elevate from those who don't. Most of us are less consistent than we think, especially in matching our actions to our identity and beliefs. The real challenge is building the awareness to see the mirror when it shows up and then having the discipline and consistency to act in alignment with who you say you are.

Here are the best places for you to learn more about Jaime Elizondo:

Follow the QR code to the Resources Page,
where you can watch the entire interview
Website: www.JaimeElizondo.com
Follow on Instagram: @Coach_Elizondo

Jamie Miller

International Keynote Speaker, Communication Coach

Jamie Miller is an international keynote speaker, communication coach, and the founder of *Art of Conscious Communication*, where he helps leaders, teams, and organizations elevate how they connect, communicate, and lead. With decades of experience in leadership development and human behavior, Jamie is known for creating clarity in complex conversations and helping people build trust, alignment, and accountability through intentional communication.

Jamie's work is grounded in the belief that communication is less about technique and more about awareness, intention, and presence. He helps leaders recognize how unconscious patterns and emotional reactions shape outcomes, teaching them how to listen deeply, speak with purpose, and lead from alignment rather than reactivity. Through keynotes, coaching, and immersive experiences, Jamie equips individuals to strengthen culture, navigate challenges, and use communication as a powerful tool for growth and transformation.

Impactful Quote from the Interview:

"I'm prepared to sleep under a bridge before I'll ever go and work for someone again. Nate, I think anyone who's got cracked lenses and is stuck working in a corporate programming environment has to change to this mentality in order to escape. They can't go into it knowing they can always go back and work in corporate if it doesn't work out. I don't buy into that notion. There can't be a plan B. I'm either going to fly to the moon or I'm going to end up under a

bridge. Once you do something with conviction for a long enough time frame, then under the bridge doesn't become your reality."

Encouragement for You from the Interview:

Taking the leap will always be the hardest part, especially when the people who care about you most are the ones asking you not to. Their concerns usually come from love and fear, not from a clear vision of what's possible for you. You don't need everyone's approval to move forward; you need alignment and the courage to begin. Once you step in, your perspective will change, your capacity will grow, and the goals you once thought were enough will naturally expand.

Along the way, you'll learn, recalibrate, and outgrow old limits, and some relationships may shift as a result. That's part of the process. The people meant to stay won't compete with you, envy you, or try to hold you back; they'll simply let you do your thing. Trust that if you're willing to take the leap, do the work, and stay authentic, clarity, confidence, and respect will catch up in time.

Challenge for You from the Interview:

Instead of asking what you want to accomplish this year, ask what your future self will thank you for, and build your life around that answer. Identify your non-negotiables and protect what makes you authentic, happy, and sustainable. Create habits that don't rely on motivation but become part of who you are, like brushing your teeth. Look at your calendar honestly and make sure it reflects your values, not constant pressure or exhaustion. Meet people where they're at, enjoy the life you're building, and remember, you don't have to choose between success and happiness.

You can have both.

Here are the best places for you to learn more about Jamie Miller:

Follow the QR code to the **Resources Page,**
where you can watch the entire interview
Website: www.artofconsciouscommunication.com
Follow on Instagram: @consciousjamie

Kristen Butler

Founder and CEO of the Power of Positivity,
Bestselling Author, Speaker, and Coach

Kristen Butler is a bestselling author, speaker, coach, and the founder & CEO of Power of Positivity, a global mindset community with over 50 million followers dedicated to helping people live happier, more joyful, and purpose-filled lives.

After hitting rock bottom, facing depression, burnout, and loss, Kristen transformed her life through positive thinking, gratitude, and self-trust. This turned her journey into a mission to uplift others. She is the author of best-selling journals and books like *The 3 Minute Positivity Journal* and *The Comfort Zone*, reframing how people understand growth and inner fulfillment.

Kristen speaks internationally on the power of positivity, mindset transformation, and how to expand one's comfort zone to create a life of flow and ease. Her life of impact has demonstrated that you can transform your life when you train your mind for more.

Impactful Quote from the Interview:

"I just thought, I don't know if I can actually get out of this… It was who I was surrounding myself with and who I was listening to. I was taking their advice internally and thinking that I needed to change, but really, I needed to be who I really am and do it unapologetically. And so I don't care if anyone's annoyed by how encouraging I can be, or positive I can be, or how much I like healthy food. I'm going to be who I am, and I'm going to attract the right people who

are also encouraged by those things and encouraged by those types of people. Just be yourself, and you'll find the right people."

Encouragement for You from the Interview:

Always question your belief systems, especially the negative ones, because very often they aren't true. Many of the beliefs we carry were picked up in childhood or passed down by well-meaning friends or family, and they may not even be ours. As we get older, we have the opportunity to evaluate those beliefs and choose new ones we actually love. That's how we begin to rewire our lives, one thought at a time. You don't have to change everything at once; sometimes changing just one belief can shift your entire lens and create a more positive way of living.

Challenge for You from the Interview:

A powerful challenge is to notice whether you're creating from a place of survival or from a place of safety. When growth is driven by anxiety and pressure, it often leads to burnout or building something that isn't truly aligned. But when action comes from internal peace and a sense of safety, the momentum feels sustainable and meaningful, even when you're working hard and stretching beyond your comfort zone. Real expansion happens when we grow from a regulated, grounded place, where how it feels inside matters just as much as what we're building.

Here are the best places for you to learn more about Kristen Butler:

Follow the QR code to the Resources Page,
where you can watch the entire interview

Website: www.PositiveKristen.com
Follow on Instagram: @PositiveKristen

Laura Casselman

CEO of JVzoo, Inc 5000 Award X5,

Best-Selling Author, International Speaker, Former Rocket

Laura Casselman is a five-time Inc. 5000 award-winning CEO, Wall Street Journal best-selling author, and the CEO and co-owner of JVZoo. Known for her ability to scale companies with intention and integrity, Laura brings a rare blend of discipline, creativity, and strategic leadership shaped by both business and performance. Before entering the world of entrepreneurship, she was a professional dancer and former Rockette—an experience that instilled the precision, resilience, and commitment to excellence that now define her leadership style.

As the author of *Trust Your Increments*, Laura teaches leaders how sustainable growth is built through consistent, intentional progress rather than shortcuts or burnout. Through her work at JVZoo and beyond, she helps entrepreneurs and organizations build trust-based cultures, align vision with execution, and scale in ways that honor both performance and people. Grounded, driven, and deeply values-oriented, Laura Casselman empowers others to pursue growth that lasts, one intentional increment at a time.

Impactful Quote from the Interview:

"No dream and no big win come without the work and the discipline. The pain and the giving up of something else in order for it to happen is required… Success without the work isn't realistic. Big accomplishments come with big sacrifices."

Encouragement for You from the Interview:

Big dreams can feel overwhelming, so don't try to tackle the whole thing at once. Break the dream into a smaller, manageable piece and make a plan to accomplish it. Reverse engineer the goal, write it out, and break it down by months, weeks, and then daily actions. Commit to doing a few intentional things each day that move you closer. As you follow the plan, you'll start proving to yourself what you're capable of, and that confidence compounds. Stop trying to impress everyone else and focus on impressing yourself. When you do, you'll realize you can accomplish far more than you ever thought possible.

Challenge for You from the Interview:

Challenge yourself to step away from social media for 30 days and redirect that time toward your next goal. Instead of spending five or ten minutes scrolling through other people's wins, use those same moments to work on what you're building. Imagine what could change in 30 days if your attention went into progress instead of comparison. Even a few focused minutes a day can create momentum, and the results might surprise you.

Here are the best places for you to learn more about Laura Casselman:

Follow the QR code to the Resources Page,
where you can watch the entire interview
Website: www.LauraCasselman.com
Follow on Instagram: @TheLauraCasselman

Michael Willett

CEO/Founder of WalkOn Nation, Former Division 1 Athlete

Michael Willett is the founder and CEO of WalkOn Nation, an organization dedicated to redefining athletic identity and helping athletes thrive beyond the game. A former Division I football player at the University of Central Florida, Michael earned his place on the team as a walk-on, an experience that shaped his resilience, work ethic, and leadership. His commitment on and off the field also helped him secure a significant academic scholarship, reinforcing the importance of excellence beyond athletics.

After a career-ending injury abruptly ended his playing days, Michael faced the difficult transition many athletes experience when the game is no longer available. Rather than letting that setback define him, he turned it into a mission. Through WalkOn Nation, Michael equips athletes with the mindset, identity, and life skills needed to navigate transition, build purpose, and succeed long after sports. His work empowers athletes to understand that while sports may be what they do, it is not who they are—and that their greatest impact often begins after the final whistle.

Impactful Quote from the Interview:

"I felt like I had to take the brunt and be the one who continues the legacy of the Willett name. So everything I did was in line with making sure the name has something to be remembered by. Recently, though, I realized that no matter what happens, I have to focus on myself first. Without focusing on myself first, everything else crumbles. I can't pull anyone with me until my chain is broken. And I realized in order to break the chain, I have to be the one who snaps it off. I can't depend on anyone else to do it. So I have to worry

about my legacy. Outside of my family's legacy, I have to worry about what I want to leave behind in life."

Encouragement for You from the Interview:

Don't let anyone change who you are, no matter where they want to pull you. You will be fine as long as you trust who you're meant to be. The best way to live is to be authentic while trusting yourself.

Challenge for You from the Interview:

The real challenge is to stop running from pain and face it head-on. Embrace those pain points, deal with them, and fight to overcome them, because when trauma and pain are avoided, the cycle only returns stronger. Look at yourself in the mirror and take accountability for your part, even when it's uncomfortable. That may mean owning some decisions, extending forgiveness, or letting go of what you've been carrying. It's hard work, but choosing accountability and forgiveness is what ultimately brings freedom from the pain you're feeling.

Here are the best places for you to learn more about Michael Willett:

Follow the QR code to the Resources Page,
where you can watch the entire interview
Website: www.WalkOnNation.org
Follow on Instagram: @WalkOn_Nation

Rebecca Black

Founder of Confidology®, Keynote Speaker, Coach

Rebecca Hatch Black is the founder of Confidology®, a framework dedicated to the daily practice and study of confidence. With nearly two decades in the beauty, wellness, and personal development industries, Rebecca has coached entrepreneurs, creatives, and executives through moments of reinvention, burnout, and breakthrough.

Her work focuses on helping high-performers stop living in the lowercase land of "fine" and step into the uppercase version of F.I.N.E. living, leadership, and impact. Rebecca's approach blends psychology, storytelling, personal experience, and practical tools to help people reconnect to who they are, not just what they do.

Impactful Quote from the Interview:

"Difficult life stories are like rainstorms… What do they do? They pass. You can handle them in one of three ways. You can try to outrun them, but they're eventually going to catch you. You can be like a cow, and you can just lie down and let it stay however long it's going to stay over you, and you just play victim. Or you can be like the buffalo; you can see the storm coming. You walk right into it and actually shorten the amount of time that you're in that season of the storm. The buffalo continues to walk through the storm even as the lightning is cracking all around them because they just want to get to the other side."

Encouragement for You from the Interview:

Remind yourself daily, "I believe I am capable of achieving great things today." That belief matters because when you choose to believe you're capable, you shift out of being stuck and into creativity. You activate the part of your mind that solves problems, finds options, and creates momentum. Belief moves you from sitting in the struggle to stepping into possibility, and that's where progress and greatness begin.

Challenge for You from the Interview:

Challenge yourself to look in the mirror every morning before you do anything else and make a choice. Tell yourself, "I choose to make a positive impact today, and I choose to be happy today." Not because you always feel happy or motivated—most days you won't—but because those choices matter. There will be mornings when you don't feel like going deep, showing up, making the call, attending the event, or doing the hard things. That's exactly why the choice has to come first.

When you commit to making an impact and choosing happiness daily, something shifts. You begin to build unshakable confidence, not from how you feel, but from how you show up. Serving others, helping someone move forward, and bringing energy into their life has a way of coming back to you. Your happiness starts to rub off, your confidence grows, and momentum follows, one intentional day at a time.

Here are the best places for you to learn more about Rebecca Black:

Follow the QR code to the Resources Page,
where you can watch the entire interview
Follow on Instagram: @becca__black

Renee Marino

International Keynote Speaker, Best-Selling Author,

Communications Expert

Renee Marino is a sought-after speaker, communication coach, former actress, and Broadway performer best known for her role as Mary Delgado in the Tony Award–winning musical Jersey Boys. After achieving success on stage and screen, Renee's career was unexpectedly derailed when she lost her singing voice, forcing her to confront identity, confidence, and purpose beyond performance. That pivotal season became the catalyst for her work today, helping others find, trust, and use their voice with clarity and authenticity.

Renee now works with leaders, entrepreneurs, and organizations to strengthen communication, emotional intelligence, and connection. Through keynotes, coaching, and workshops, she teaches practical tools for presence, listening, self-expression, and courageous communication, whether on stage, in meetings, and in everyday conversations. Known for her warmth, honesty, and real-world insight, Renee empowers people to stop performing who they think they should be and start showing up as who they truly are, using their voice as a powerful tool for leadership, impact, and meaningful relationships.

Impactful Quote from the Interview:

"Some of the most talented people in the world end up leaving the business not because they're not talented enough but because of those cracked lenses. Those broken dreams are there because of the cracks in the foundation that they let get in. That's why it's so important to have a strong support system. We are

*meant to connect, we are meant to help one another,
and we are meant to lift each other up.”*

Encouragement for You from the Interview:

Be gentler with yourself and stop judging yourself; self-judgment is one of the worst things we carry. Infuse more joy into what you're doing and remember that this isn't the end-all, be-all. Life is about the journey; "the juice is in the journey." You don't have to be perfect or hide the parts where you're still learning. Trial and error isn't failure; it's part of how you grow and how you're meant to experience life. Give yourself permission to show up fully, imperfections and all, and let joy be part of the process.

Challenge for You from the Interview:

Take imperfect action. Do it when you're afraid. Do it when you're confused. Do it when you don't know what the next five steps are. Take imperfect action. Take the leap and have faith the net will appear.

Here are the best places for you to learn more about Renee Marino:

Follow the QR code to the Resources Page,
where you can watch the entire interview
Website: www.reneemarino.com
Follow on Instagram: @IamReneeMarino

Ted Rath

Director of Sports Performance - New Orleans Saints,
Best Selling Author, Keynote Speaker

Ted Rath is a nationally recognized leader in elite performance, culture, and leadership with more than 16 years of experience across the NFL. He currently serves as Director of Sports Performance for the New Orleans Saints, where he leads high-performance strategy focused on health, longevity, and competitive excellence at the highest level of professional football.

Previously, Ted served as Vice President of Player Performance for the Philadelphia Eagles, helping guide the organization to a Super Bowl appearance and earning NFL Strength and Conditioning Coach of the Year honors for the second time in his career. Over the years, he has directed performance departments for the Eagles, Rams, Dolphins, and Lions, consistently building resilient, healthy, and high-performing teams. Beyond the field, Ted is the best-selling author of *Beyond Comfort* and a trusted voice in leadership and culture development for organizations in both sports and business. His work is rooted in the belief that true performance is built through discipline, purpose, and care for the whole person, bringing hope and strength to those navigating challenges and adversity.

Impactful Quote from the Interview:

"When those hard times hit, when those dark days come after me, what I tell myself is this: Do your habits of today align with your goals of tomorrow? It doesn't matter if I want to get up and be a great leader one day. It doesn't matter if I want to get up at 4 a.m. and attack work with passion, with energy,

with integrity, with all the things I know I need to make a positive difference. But when I ask myself, do your habits of today align with your goals of tomorrow, it snaps me into that moment where I have to get up and do the work. This is my opportunity. And especially on those days, the challenging days where you don't want to do it, that's when you make a difference."

Encouragement for You from the Interview:

Give yourself grace when you make a mistake, but don't give yourself excuses. Excuses can lead to entitlement and enablement, while grace allows you to learn and grow. Many of us are our own hardest coaches, quick to beat ourselves up when we fall short. Instead of running from failure or feeling embarrassed by it, recognize that a mistake is simply an opportunity to improve. That moment isn't a setback—it's a gift.

Grace doesn't mean avoiding the work. It means allowing yourself to fail without self-punishment, learning what the moment is teaching you, and then taking action. Build the process. Create the system. Do the work. But do it with grace, knowing that growth happens when you allow yourself to learn, adjust, and move forward stronger than before.

Challenge for You from the Interview:

One of the most important practices is to learn "Zoomability," which is to zoom out, detach, and get away from the emotional state that you're probably in. When you're emotionally "in it," staring through a cracked lens, you lose clarity. Real clarity comes when you detach, step back, and see the entire situation for what it is. Whatever chaos you're facing, a tough season, a job loss, uncertainty, zoom out and look for the opportunity. It's there, but you won't see it if you're too close to the emotion.

Once you find that clarity, you have to zoom back in just as intentionally. Identify where you can apply new systems, processes, and actions. Give yourself grace in the moment, gain perspective, then narrow your focus and go to work. Growth happens in that rhythm, zooming out for clarity, then zooming in with purpose and action.

Here are the best places for you to learn more about Ted Rath:

Follow the QR code to the Resources Page,
where you can watch the entire interview
Website: www.TedWrath.com
Follow on Instagram: @TedRathStrengthCoach

Access to All Interviews and Resources

For the resources page and to access the full interviews, use the QR code below or go to www.CrackedLensesBook.com/Resources

Scan the QR Code Here: